Existentialism and Christian Zen

An East/West Way to Christ

Existentialism and Christian Zen

An East/West Way to Christ

A William McVey

Winchester, UK
Washington, USA

First published by Circle Books, 2012
Circle Books is an imprint of John Hunt Publishing Ltd., Laurel House, Station Approach,
Alresford, Hants, SO24 9JH, UK
office1@jhpbooks.net
www.johnhuntpublishing.com
www.circle-books.com

For distributor details and how to order please visit the 'Ordering' section on our website.

Text copyright: A William McVey 2011

ISBN: 978 1 78099 593 9

A CIP catalogue record for this book is available from the British Library.

Design: Stuart Davies

Printed and bound by CPI Group (UK) Ltd, Croydon, CR0 4YY

We operate a distinctive and ethical publishing philosophy in all
areas of our business, from our global network of authors to
production and worldwide distribution.

CONTENTS

Introduction

'Some years ago,' William Johnston suggests, 'Arnold Toynbee declared that when the historian of a thousand years from now comes to write the history of our time, he will be preoccupied not with the Viet Nam war, not with the struggle between capitalism and communism, not with racial strife, but with what happened when, for the first time, Christianity and Buddhism began to penetrate one another deeply' (Johnston 1979, 1). This was written by William Johnston in the late 1970s; since then, the interest in Buddhism on the part of Western theologians has grown. Johnston describes his dialogue with Buddhism from a limited perspective: 'I have called this little book *Christian Zen*, but the contents are less ambitious than the pretentious title might suggest. Rather than treating of the confluence of two vast traditions of East and West, I simply try to say something about how Zen and Christianity have met in me, setting down some practical conclusions that this meeting has evoked' (Johnston 1979, 1).

I am not interested in examining in any theological depth the meeting of the Western and Eastern mind. I approach the issue of Eastern spiritual techniques strictly as a pragmatic pastor in a postmodern culture. Furthermore, I am concerned with the finding of the calm mind in these days of anxiety. Most often, Western Christians view mysticism and meditation as a type of esoteric practice that seems strange to the ordinary person. As a pastor, it is my calling to dispel this serious misconception.

This book is divided into three sections. Part One builds on the existential awareness of no-thing and the relationship between the Zen concept of Mu and the Christian mystical practice of Via Negativa. Part Two develops the fundamental existential concept of will (volition), the practice of Christian Zen and the discovery of hope. Part Three merely lays out some suggested methods of Christian Zen style meditation.

Part One

Christian Zen, the Existential Center and No-thing

I

The Practice of Self Realization

Philip Kapleau, in the preface to *The Three Pillars of Zen*, clearly holds that:

> Briefly stated, Zen is a religion with a unique method of body-mind training whose aim is Self Realization ... At the profoundest level Zen, like every other great religion, transcends its own teachings and practices, yet at the same time there is no Zen apart from these practices. Attempts in the West to isolate Zen in a vacuum of the intellect, cut off from the very disciplines which are its raison d'etre, have nourished in places a pseudo-Zen that is little more than a mind tickling diversion. I believe that the Japanese school of Zen Buddhism has perhaps for thousands of years remained the most faithful to the original mindfulness practice of the Buddha that leads to enlightenment (satori).
>
> (Kapleau 1980, 69)

Kapleau's book is about the closest a Westerner might get to a sense of the teachings of Zen Buddhism. Even people who have practiced a combination of various forms of Eastern and Western meditation find it difficult to read. It serves to give a genuine insight into Zen, while simultaneously portraying how difficult it is for a Western left-brain person to comprehend.

Kapleau's explanation of Zen, I have found, fits well with my heart, mind and most of all my existential wondering soul. In terms of existential philosophy and therapy, we wander and worry about the lack of meaning in postmodern society. Without meaning in our life, we are driven by our anxiety-based nature and all of its manifestations in the ego. In existentialism, the solution to our anxiety-driven wandering is found by reaching into the deepest elements of humanity. When we explore our being, the existentialist always returns to the core person that recognizes a call to live courageously:

> A chief characteristic of this courage is that it requires centeredness within our own being, without which we would feel ourselves to be a vacuum. The emptiness within corresponds to an apathy without, and apathy adds up, in the long run, to cowardice. This is why we must always base our commitment in the center of our own being, or else no commitment will be ultimately authentic ... Courage is not a virtue or value among other personal values like love or fidelity. It is the foundation that underlies and gives reality to all other virtues and personal values. Without courage our fidelity becomes conformism.
> (May 1975, 13)

In an existential analysis, our higher power is the discovery of mind.

Kapleau explains Zen as a religious practice. He does not say religious beliefs or institutions; rather it is a religious practice. It is a religious practice because in Zen there is a belief in the dharma, i.e. the proven way of Zen. Furthermore, Zen has a faith in the power of satori (enlightenment); in other words, it has a belief in the higher mind. In Zen, like existentialism, there is no unconscious mind; there is only the mind. If you ask a true Zen master where the mind is, then he will tell you, 'The mind is where you focus.' In Zen, there is a salvific belief in the discovery of the 'Original Mind.' It is where we go to find our true nature, and it is by means of our Original Mind that we find the solution to pain, suffering and anxiety:

> If you would free yourself of the sufferings of samsara (the

law of causation), you must learn the direct way to become a Buddha. This way is no other than the realization of your own mind. Now what is this mind? It is the true nature of all sentient beings, that which existed before our parents were born. This mind is intrinsically pure. When we are born, it is not newly created, and when we die, it does not perish. It has no distinction of male or female, nor has it any coloration of good or bad. It cannot be compared with anything, so it is called Buddha nature. Yet countless thoughts issue from this self-nature as waves arise in the ocean or as images are reflected in the mirror.

To realize your own mind you must first of all look into the source from which thoughts flow. Sleeping and working, standing and sitting, profoundly ask yourself, 'What is my own mind?' with an intense yearning to resolve this question. This is called 'training' or 'practice' or 'desire for truth' or 'thirst for realization.'

(Kapleau 1980, 193)

2

The Existential Center

What we have here from the perspective of an existential analysis is the courageous pursuit of meaning that awaits us at the center of our existence. Perhaps the existential core that is discovered in contemplation, art, music and poetry is somewhat similar to this Zen Mind. It takes a courageous effort of time and practice to come to enlightenment and belief in the dharma of the 'Original Mind.' It takes a courageous belief in the teachings of the Zen masters to trust them and enter on the journey to the Original Mind. In Zen, the true self is like the moon that cannot be seen because it is covered by the clouds. The Zen clouds are the three delusions of anger, greed and ignorance.

Anxiety is a combination of thoughts and feelings that comes from the ego driven by the need for self-esteem, affluence and the lack of courage to look for our true self. The three delusions clearly address the issue of anxiety and removing the anxiety clouds that keep us from the Original Mind. It has been my experience over the years as a pastor that anxiety and anger always go together. Why are people who have so much affluence in their life so angry? Why do Western Christians become increasingly angry at non-believers and the world? Why is anger and intolerance increasing? Anxiety is the driving emotion of the angry ego, and we fight in vain against anger with left-brain practices of rational insight and preaching. The overcoming of anger in Zen is achieved with the practice of Zazen.

In the gospels, we meet a gut Jesus who fearlessly confronts the inner demonic voices of anxiety. Christians are often afraid of getting to the gut where it is messy because we look for a nice Jesus. When we read the gospels, most often Jesus presents us with ambiguities and paradoxes. Johnston writes,

Zen is meant to drive conviction down into the guts. Here it is in contrast with Western prayer, which for the past couple of centuries has tended to be very cerebral and has not rooted itself deeply in the personality, with the result that many Christians, even nuns and priests, can jettison long held convictions in moments of emotional crisis. Probably they would not be able to do this if their convictions were lodged at the gut level through Zen.

(Johnston 1979, 34)

The practice of Zazen is to bring a follower a life of mindfulness. Being present is the meaning of mindfulness, and being present for Zen is living in the state of awareness. The key of Zen Buddhism is that the seeds of enlightenment are sown in mindful living.

It will be fair to say that 'presence' is the cornerstone of all true spirituality, regardless of ethnic or cultural origin. Presence is something that Jesus emphasized over and over again. The Gospels are filled with statements of Jesus that begin with words like 'Beware' (be aware), 'Look,' 'Hear and understand …' In this sense, the teaching of Jesus is very close to that of the Buddha. After all, Buddhism is a culture of awareness. The word 'Buddha,' for example, means the 'Awakened One.' Similarly Jesus is called 'The Light of the World' in the Gospel of John. In the Sermon on the Mount, Jesus alerted his disciples to the importance of awareness, 'The eye is the lamp of the body. So, if your eye is sound, your whole body will be full of light; but if your eye is not sound, your whole body will be full of darkness. If the light in you is darkness how great is the darkness!' (Matt. 6:22–23).

(Leong 1995, 48)

From the teaching of Jesus and the Buddha, we learn that 'Being

Present in a state of Awareness' is the foundation of the spiritual life both in Buddhism and Christianity.

3

No-thing

As an existential Christian, I am particularly drawn to the practice of Zen and the method of Zazen by the concept of Mu.

A monk came to Joshu, a renowned Zen master in China hundreds of years ago, and asked: 'has a dog a Buddha nature or not?' Joshu retorted, 'Mu!' Literally the expression means 'no' or 'nothing,' but the significance of Joshu's answer does not lie in the word. Mu is the expression of the living, functioning, dynamic Buddha-nature. What you must do is discover the spirit or essence of this Mu, not through intellectual analysis but search into your innermost being. Then you must demonstrate before me, concretely and vividly, that you understand Mu as living truth, without recourse to conceptions, theories, or abstract explanations. Remember, you can't understand Mu through ordinary cognition; you must grasp it directly with your whole being.

(Kapleau 1980, 152)

Here in the Zen teaching of Mu that the master explains to the student we face a similar issue in existential philosophy and therapy, and it is the issue of being and non-being. *Irrational Man* by William Barrett, *A Study in Existential Philosophy*, was published in 1958. Like many existential writings of the fifties and sixties, it is most applicable to the current state of Western culture and the American dream that has plunged into a deeply experienced age of anxiety. Barrett in this work gives a rather brilliant and concise analysis of the existential movement and its major philosophers, and the major themes of the Western existential movement, namely the phenomenon of nothingness (or, as the Zen master explains it, no-thing): 'This philosophy embodies the self-questioning of the time, seeking to reorient itself to its own destiny. Indeed, the whole problematic of Existentialism unfolds from the historical fragility and contingency of human life; the impotence of reason confronted with the depths of existence; the threat of Nothingness, and the solitary and unsheltered condition of the individual before the threat' (Barrett 1958, 36).

Existentialism argues that it is no longer possible in an age of anxiety, by means of Western dogmatic and fundamental biblical language, to enter into the divine. Also, an understanding of truth, the future of the universe and global ethics is no longer achievable by means of the principles and methods of the traditional Cartesian method of science. This view of science finds no place for the subjective and emotive approach to truth; rather it leads to a world that is mechanical and grasped only through the propositions of left-brain mathematical and empirical observation. Gradually, without an existential perspective view of man and the universe, humanity is doomed to run feverishly from its increasing sense of anxiety.

In Heidegger Nothingness is a presence within our own Being, always there, in the inner quaking that goes on beneath the calm surface of our preoccupation with things. Anxiety before Nothingness has many modalities and guises: now trembling and creative, now panicky and destructive; but always it is as inseparable from ourselves as our own breathing because anxiety is our existence itself in its radical insecurity. In anxiety, we both are and are not, at one and the same time, and this is our dread. Our finitude is such that positive and negative interpenetrate our whole existence.
    (Barrett 1958, 226)

Zen Buddhism is fully aware of the existential situation of

anxiety being as close as our very own breath, but it is here Zen finds the solution in its approach to the pain and suffering of our anxiety-based existence. It is in the contemplative focus on the no-thing, and this focus must occur in the practice of meditative silence. It is here that we find another link with Heidegger who breaks away from the traditional Western view of truth and organizes all his thoughts under the categories, similar to Buddhist psychology, of 1) moods and feelings, 2) understanding, 3) speech. That is, we know life not by the Aristotelian and analytical logical qualitative and quantitative categories. We know life and the meaning of truth by our moods and feelings, how we understand these moods and feelings and how we express them in speech. 'Language, for Heidegger, is not primarily a system of sounds or of marks on paper symbolizing those sounds. Sounds and marks upon paper can become language only because man, in so far as he exists, stands within language' (Barrett 1958, 221). William Barrett describes Heidegger in terms most acceptable to a student of Zen Buddhism: 'This looks very paradoxical; but, as with the rest of Heidegger, to understand what he means we have to cast off our usual habits of thought and let ourselves see what the thing is – i.e. let the thing itself be seen rather than riding roughshod over it with readymade conceptions.' Is this not similar to the Zen master who teaches that the pursuit of Mu (no-thing) leads us to grasp reality with the whole mind in itself without conceptions, theories and abstract explanations?

There is also in Heidegger another element essential to the pursuit of meaning by a humanity torn between being and non-being, i.e. the basic ontological nature; it is the language of silence. Barrett explains:

Two people are talking together. They understand each other, and they fall silent – a long silence. This silence is language; it may speak more eloquently than any words. In their mode, they are attuned to each other; they may even reach down into that understanding which, as we have seen above, lies below articulation. This significant, speaking silence shows that sounds or marks do not constitute the essence of language. Nor is this silence merely a gap in our chatter; it is, rather, the primordial attunement of one existent to another, out of which language – as sounds, marks, and counters – comes. It is only because man is capable of such silence that he is capable of authentic speech. If he ceases to be rooted in that silence all this talk becomes chatter.

(Barrett 1958, 223)

Zen Buddhism and existentialism are in a very real sense a nihilist view of life. It is an explanation of life in the book of Ecclesiastes 1:2:

'Meaningless, Meaningless!'
says the Teacher.
'Utterly meaningless!
Everything is meaningless.'
(NIV)

The word for 'meaningless' can also be translated as 'breath' or 'vapor,' but it is basically a nihilist spiritual view. However, similar to the Zen 'Mu' and Heidegger's language of silence, it is a constructive nihilism. Again, it is William Barrett who eloquently explains the nature of this constructive mystical nothingness:

As a matter of fact, human moods and reactions to the encounter with Nothingness vary considerably from person to person and from culture to culture. The Chinese Taoists found the Great Void tranquilizing, peaceful, and even joyful. For the Buddhists in India, the idea of No-thing evoked a mood of universal compassion for all creatures caught in the toils of an existence that is ultimately groundless. In the traditional culture of Japan the idea of Nothingness pervades the exquisite modes of aesthetic feeling displayed in painting, architecture, and even the ceremonial rituals of daily life. But Western man, up to his neck in things, objects, and the business of mastering them, recoils with anxiety from any possible encounter with Nothingness and labels talk of it as 'negative' – which is to say, morally reprehensible. Clearly, then, the moods with which men react to this Nothing vary according to time, place, and cultural conditioning; but what is at issue here is not the mood with which one ought to confront such a presence, but the reality of the presence itself.

(Barrett 1958, 285)

4

Christian Mysticism

This mystical nihilistic knowledge is also discovered in the history of Christian mysticism. It is boldly articulated by a Syrian monk who lived at the end of the fifth century. The identity of Dionysius the Areopagite, or, as he is often called, the Pseudo-Dionysius, is unknown. This monk ascribed his works to Dionysius the Areopagite who was a friend of Saint Paul, and addressed them to Paul's fellow worker, Timothy. He is thought to have been a contemporary of the Apostle Paul, and his writings, at the time, were given the same authority as those of the New Testament.

Supernal Triad, Deity above all essence, knowledge and goodness; Guide of Christians of Divine Wisdom; direct our path to the ultimate summit of Thy mystical Lore, most incomprehensible, most luminous, and most exalted, where the pure, absolute, and immutable mysteries of theology are veiled in the dazzling obscurity of the secret Silence, outshining all brilliance with the intensity of their Darkness, and surcharging our blinded intellects with the utterly impalpable and invisible fairness of glories surpassing all beauty.

Let this be my prayer; but do thou, dear Timothy, in the diligent exercise of the mystical contemplation, leave behind the senses and the operations of the intellect, and all things sensible and intellectual, and all things in the world of being and non-being, that thou mayest arise, by unknowing, towards the union, as far as attainable, with Him Who transcends all being and all knowledge. For by the unceasing and absolute renunciation of thyself and of all things, thou mayest be borne on high through pure and entire self abnegation, into the superessential Radiance of the Divine Darkness.

(Happold 1963, 212)

Here we have an expression of the earliest mysticism of the Christian church that follows a similar path of nothingness as that of the existential quest and the Zen teaching of Mu. It is a nihilistic spirituality that leads in Zen to the enlightenment of the Original Mind, in Christian mysticism to the love and radiance of the Divine Darkness, and in existential philosophy-psychology to freedom from anxiety, by the acceptance of the state of being and non-being as a call to the self, or as the metaphysical poet Eliot calls it, the Third Name (our true identity).

I hope that I have not been overly intellectual, because the purpose of this work is to explore methods of calmness in an age of anxiety. I am, however, a Christian pastor, and I believe that Christian practice must have metaphysical, mystical heft. We are able to discover a mystical theology in an experimental wisdom stretching out to God expressed by the restless desire of the soul for divine love. Goethe really described this heft in terms of a mystical theology as the scholastic of the heart, the dialectic of the feelings. Mystical metaphysical heft is sometimes called by scholars like Henri Bergson an intellectual intuition, an intellectual sympathy or formless speculation. Following the teachers of mystical metaphysical heft, I have outlined the path of Zen Mu and the existential quest for overcoming anxiety by the discovery of the courageous self.

These paths of mystical metaphysics require an acceptance of spiritual nihilism. One of the finest expressions of the nihilist road to God and the calmness of self-discovery in our life is found in the teaching of the Spanish mystics of the twelfth century. Their teaching and practice is presented in the work by Gerald G. May, M.D., *The Awakened Heart*, where he discusses the mysticism of Teresa of Avila and John of the Cross:

Our sense seeks beauty, the sweetness, and the good feelings of God. Our mind seeks the truth and wisdom of God. Our will seeks to live out the goodness, the righteousness of God. In other words, we yearn for the attributes of God with every part of ourselves. Human beings are two legged, walking, talking desires for God.

Ultimately, it is only God's very self that can truly satisfy our deepest desires; our capacities are limited in what they can apprehend, and God's true nature is always beyond them. The best they can do is reflect some image or concept of God, some brief glimpse seen 'through a glass darkly' (1 Cor. 13:12). God is at once too immanently at one with us and too transcendently beyond us to be fully felt or appreciated in any normal way ... God's true attributes are too perfect, too pure, and too delicate for any of our faculties to grasp.

To put it another way, all our capacities are geared toward appreciating objects of attention, sense perceptions, images, ideas, memories, emotions, fantasies, and so on. But God is too intimate to be an object, too ultimate to be a thing. Our faculties can only comprehend the things of God, like the beauty of creation, the goodness of the attraction we feel for others, or the glimpses of truth we experience in religious images and concepts. All these things may reflect or represent God to us, but they miss the essence of God. To our normal human capacities God is nada, no-thing.

(May 1991, 174)

Thomas Merton, the well-known Trappist and mystical author, once wrote to William Johnston about the use of Zen and the pursuit of satori, meaning enlightenment. In order to appreciate his response, it is important to realize that Merton in his later life had begun to pursue the practices of Eastern meditation and particularly Zen. He did, however, continually return to his own Catholic mysticism with a sense of having discovered anew its deep value and similarity with the Zen tradition. In a sense, he seems to see the value of Zen as allowing us to develop a more down-to-earth type of mystical awareness in this information age. He writes, 'Probably the best thing to do is to use Zen for purposes of inner purification and liberation from system and conceptual thinking without bothering about whether or not we get *satori*' (Johnston 1979, 22).

William Johnston, in *Christian Zen: A Way of Meditation*, writes:

The Judaeo-Christian tradition, as is well known, is extremely theocentric. Everything hinges on God. This stems in large measure from the Bible, where all is attributed to the guiding hand of Yahweh. If the rain falls, this is the work of Yahweh. If someone goes astray, Yahweh hardens his heart. If he dies, Yahweh strikes him down. And so on. This is all the more stressed in the communication of God to man: the great experience of Abraham, Moses, and Paul had nothing whatever to do with their own efforts, their own asceticism, their own prayer. All was the gift of Yahweh ... As opposed to this view, Zen is extremely man-centered and existential. You are simply to sit and get on with the job. The instructions are concerned with your spine and your eyes and your abdomen; in a very practical way you are led to Samadhi (intense yet effortless concentration) without too much theory. What you are asked to believe is that you possess the Buddha nature and that enlightenment is possible. Here is something for Christianity. Terminology about acquired and infused contemplation, about ordinary and extraordinary prayer, about gratia gratis and gratia faciens – all these complications can quietly and conveniently be dropped. They aren't really necessary, because the experience itself is frightfully simple and uncomplicated. In my opinion we could even dispense with the word contemplation and put in its place 'Christian samadhi.' This would have the good effect of bringing us into line with other spiritual traditions which use the word. Besides, contemplation is a Latin word, translation of the Greek theoria. Must Christians forever stick to the Hellenistic vocabulary?

(Johnston 1979, 46)

At the heart of any form of Christian existentialism is the emphasis placed on the volitional nature of man. God has created us free human beings who have the ever present option of saying yes or no to our inner Christ nature. When we enter into Christian mindfulness, we say yes to Christ, and we participate in the energy of the Spirit. It is by entering into this 'Yes' that we exercise the fundamental act of our spiritual being, thereby affirming our Godly sense of being. This is called man's fundamental option as to whether a person wishes to accept spiritual meaning into their life. For Christians it means a willingness to discover our Christ nature. When I teach classes on Christian Zen I teach the three beliefs of Buddhism, i.e. 'I take refuge in the Buddha; I take refuge in the Dharma (the way); I take refuge in the Sangha (my spiritual companions).' I then explain that we will change these three beliefs to: 'I take refuge in the Christ nature; I take refuge in the way of Christ; I take refuge in my spiritual community.'

In order to explain more deeply and at a level of comfort for Christian practitioners of Zen that Zazen is compatible with the Christian faith, I find it is necessary to give attention to the tradition and teachings of the Orthodox Christian Church. Eastern Orthodox thinking is more compatible with the practices of Zen than Roman Catholicism or the Reformed Church. It is grounded on the mystical base of its prominent mystical theologians. In Orthodox theology, Aristotelian thought, as it influenced Thomas Aquinas and Roman Catholicism, is absent. It is particularly in the Orthodox theology of the Trinity and grace where the mystical is discovered. Orthodox theology is equated with mystical experiences. Consequently, in the Eastern Orthodox Church, union with God is seen as a spiritual state attainable by far more than the contemplative saint. In Orthodox teaching, it should be the objective of all Christians to live the Christian life in its mystical fullness.

5

Via Negativa

The theology of the Orthodox Church is essentially an apophatic (negative) theology. It is grounded on the incomprehensibility of God. The nature of God conceived as the Ultimate Reality is completely unapproachable and unknowable, beyond all that exists and all that can be thought. The question arises, therefore: How can we hope to know God? An answer is given in the works of Pseudo-Dionysius when he wrote of a 'higher faculty' of the soul through which it is possible for humanity to be united to Him who is wholly unknowable; thus by knowing nothing we come to know that which is beyond all knowledge.

Eastern theology is a theology and a spirituality that accepts that our knowledge and experience of God is always a matter of polarity and is expressed in a language of polarity. Eastern theology holds that the Divine Essence is the uncreated energies of God and the created being of man. God is made known to us created beings through the Trinity in Unity; not, however, through the essence of the Trinity which is one with the unknowable God, equally God, and therefore Itself inaccessible and unknowable, but through the uncreated energies within It. The Trinity is more than Its Essence; within the Essence, and inseparable from it, there are the uncreated Energies, in and through which it goes forth from Itself and manifests, communicates and gives itself to us.

The uncreated Energies are the exterior of God, outpouring of Itself, while still remaining Itself unchanged, into the realm of created being. The knowledge of the unknowable One by created beings is said to fall within the sphere of the divine economy. This is a difficult teaching to understand. St. Gregory of Thessalonica wrote, 'The divine nature must be said to be at the same time both exclusive of and, in some sense open to participation. We attain to participation in the divine nature, and yet at the same time it remains totally inaccessible. We need to affirm both at the same time and to preserve the antinomy as a criterion of right devotion' (Happold 1963, 219).

In the first lesson of the Book of Tao, we read a very similar concept of the divine mystery as we find in Orthodox teachings: 'The Tao that can be told is not the eternal Tao. The name that can be named is not the eternal Name. Free from desire, you realize the mystery. Caught in desire, you see only manifestations. Yet mystery and manifestations arise from the same source. This source is called darkness within darkness, and it is the gateway to all understanding' (Mitchell 1988, 1).

The Mystery and the Mysteries are inaccessible to thought (concepts and images) and only to be known by means of participation in the divine life.

6

Christian Zen and the Pentecostal Moment

The Eastern doctrine of deification teaches that by means of participatory grace, we advance towards union with God. As we advance, we grow to a higher level of consciousness. We reach a point where consciousness becomes an enlightened consciousness, and we are no longer bound to the senses. Man should be able to attain union with God by means of grace, but man must also play his part and work towards enlightenment and transformation. A widely recognized practice in Orthodox mysticism is through the Prayer of Jesus.

The words of the prayer are simple: 'Lord Jesus Christ, Son of God, have mercy on me, a sinner.' It is more than a petition prayer; it is really almost a scientific attempt to change the one who prays. Spiritual directors give precise directions on how the prayer should be used and prayed.

1 It is said aloud a specific number of times each day in quiet solitude.
2 It is repeated silently throughout the day and at night.
3 Eventually the aspirant begins to breathe the prayer in the heart and becomes more and more aware of the divine breathing.

The Jesus Prayer is a mantra, which is a single evocative word or a sacred sentence or some form of creative sound. The sound of a mantra awakens the dormant forces in the soul.

Theophanes, known as the Recluse:

The object of our search is the fire of grace which enters into the heart ... When the spark of God Himself – grace – appears

23

in the heart, it is the prayer of Jesus which quickens it and fans it into flame. But it does not create the spark – it gives only the possibility that it may be received, by recollecting the thoughts and making ready the soul before the face of the Lord. The essential thing is to hold oneself ready before the Lord, calling out to Him from the depths of one's heart ... God is concerned with the heart.

(Happold 1963, 225)

Brianchaninov on the Prayer of Jesus:

Experience will show that in using this method (i.e. the Jesus Prayer), the words should be pronounced with extreme unhurriedness, so that the mind may be able to enter into the words as into forms ... One must train oneself as if one were reading the syllables – with the same unhurriedness.

(Happold 1963, 225)

St. Isaac the Syrian writes,

He who desires to see the Lord within himself endeavors to purify his heart by the unceasing remembrance of God. The spiritual land of a man pure in soul is within him. The sun which shines in it is the light of the Holy Trinity. The air which its inhabitant breathes is the All-Holy Spirit. The life, joy and gladness of that country is Christ, the Light of the Light – the Father. That is the Jerusalem or Kingdom of God hidden within us, according to the word of the Lord. Try to enter the cell within you, and you will see the heavenly cell. They are one and the same. By one entry you enter both. The ladder to the Heavenly Kingdom is within you. It is mysteriously in your soul.

(Happold 1963, 224)

Here we discover the mystic base of the Orthodox fathers, which is a monistic nature. By developing a discipline of Christian Zen-like mindfulness, it becomes possible to experience God as the inner Christ, thereby ceasing to treat God as an object outside of ourselves.

Western Christianity has become an awareness of God in terms of dualism. In traditional Western Catholic and Reformation spirituality, God is the totally other who comes to us as a person totally broken and separated from God. Consequently, God is always coming to us from the outside, meaning that we come to God as an object separate from our existence. The problem is that if God is always coming to us from the totally other perspective, it is not possible to have a true existential relationship with God. It is the ever present problem in Western theology and spirituality of 'the one and the many' that we have inherited since the time of Aristotle and Aquinas.

We can look at the universe and our participation in the universe in one of two ways: either there is one thing or there are many things. Common-sense everyday life tells us that there are many things, but science steadily begins to look for the famous drive of physics, which is a total explanation of everything in terms of the basic energy structure of the universe. Zen, like science, has always taught that there is only one thing. This one thing of Zen is silent, imageless, and without subject and object. It is the Tao. As we see from the early mystical father, we participate as part of our very existence in God's oneness. We are separate yet one in God because unto each human being has been given the Christ cell, the center within us. It is the Christ cell that comes forth when we enter into Christ-centered, Zen-like meditation.

Mindfulness, I suggest, is similar to the existential quest for being present in the world in a full state of awareness. In mystical existentialism and states of Christ mindfulness, the issue of being and non-being vanishes because we become one and the same with the divine energy of the Trinity. Jesus has come to open to us the energy of the Trinity, yet at the same time teaching us that the Godhead is separate. Eckhart taught:

> The soul must step beyond or jump past creatures if it is to know God ... I do not think the least of creatures absorb your attention, you will see nothing of God, however little that creature may be. Thus, in *Book of Love*, the soul says: 'I have run around looking for him my soul loves and found him not.' She found angels and many other things but not him that her soul loved, but she goes on to say: 'After that, I went a little further and found him my soul loves.' It was as if she said: 'It was when I stepped beyond creatures that I found my soul's lover.' The soul must step beyond or jump past creatures if it is to know God.
>
> (Happold 1963, 274)

When we enter into deep states of mindful silence, we realize that the Christ cell begins to move throughout our mind and body. In Christian states of Zen likeness, the movement is felt and known, and it leads to an excitation of the Spirit. It is what Christians know as the Pentecostal moment similar to when the Spirit comes to Jesus in the gospel scene with John the Baptist. Perhaps the teachings and practice of Christian Zen offer us a new way of understanding the meaning of the Pentecostal experience.

Part Two

Zen, the Existential Will and the Soul

7

Christian Hope and the Existential Horizon

There are two schools of existential philosophy, namely theistic and atheistic. However, there are two major beliefs that both expressions of existentialism share. One, the meaning of life comes from human experiences and our reflection on these experiences in our struggle to define our place in this universe. Two, the existentialist finds meaning based on the discovering of possibilities offered by life and the courage to express the unique sense of self.

Even one of the best-known existential philosophers, Jean-Paul Sartre, claims there is a common belief to the atheistic and theistic view of meaning and the striving for the best life:

> What complicates matters is that there are two kinds of existentialism; first, those who are Christians, among whom I would include Jaspers and Gabriel Marcel, both Catholic; and on the other hand the atheistic existentialists, among whom I class Heidegger, and the French existentialists and myself. What they have in common is that existence precedes essence, or if you prefer, that subjectivity must be the starting point.
> (Sartre 1957, 12–13)

The title of this work expresses an effort in theistic existentialism that more specifically is a Christian existentialism in dialogue with Zen Buddhism.

Existentialism is an action-oriented view of life, and Christian existentialism is a commitment to the discovering of the authentic inner Christ self that leads to life-loving compassion and hope. Fundamentally, Christianity is a spirituality of hope: 'For the Christian, hope arises out of endurance in the face of adversity, based on trust in the love of God (Romans 5:3–5). Hope is essentially a moral commitment, for it is a good future for which we dare to hope. If that is the case, we should be prepared to work for what we hope for. Of course, human striving cannot bring about our ultimate destiny, for that lies in the hands of God, but spiritual formation can fit us for what that final destiny is hoped to be. Moreover, to the extent that hope is partially realizable within present history, it is a realization that is to be striven for. As Jürgen Moltmann says of a theology of hope, it is "a theology of combatants, and not onlookers"' (Polkinghorne 2002). Christian existentialism is grounded on a spirituality of hope. Christian spirituality in prayer and meditation is about allowing our inner Christ to open us to our existential possibilities.

The Christian Existential Horizon

A horizon is the place in the distance where the earth or the sky meets the water. It is a point where the heavenly touches the earth. It is possible by means of the Pythagorean geometric formula to measure a point on the horizon from where we are standing using the zenith, the nadir and the radiance of the horizon from our point of view. However, to properly measure the horizon we must be standing on a flat base of land or a calm sea.

God has sent His Son to teach us that life is about always looking for the spiritual horizon, as Paul teaches us in Romans:

> We know the whole creation has been groaning as in the pains of childbirth right up to the present time. Not only so, but we ourselves, who have the firstfruits of the Spirit, groan inwardly as we wait eagerly for our adoption as sons, the redemption of our bodies. For this hope we were saved. But hope that is seen is no hope at all. Who hopes for what he already has? But if we do not yet have, we wait patiently.

(Romans 8:22–25 NIV)

When we are experiencing the turmoil and storms of life, we are always able to discover hope by finding an existential horizon where we will find not only the solution to the present tension-ridden situation, but we will find a better horizon; we will find a better way to live. When we are suffering from the tensions of life, we must look for the existential horizon. We must find the place where heaven touches earth. We must find the place where God's plan touches our plan. Finding where we touch God when we are experiencing tension is the meaning of finding the existential horizon.

In order to find this existential horizon, we must use a spiritual formula, just as we do when we measure the physical horizon. We must first get to a flat, solid base that allows us to see the emerging apparent horizon. The basic ingredient of 'existential horizon' thinking is to call forth God's gift of tranquility and serenity. In order to find the new horizons in the midst of turmoil, we must stand on the solid base of a serene mind. James Allen, the great spiritual writer of the Industrial Revolution, beautifully describes the power of a serene mind and soul:

Tempest-tossed souls, wherever ye may be, under whatever conditions ye may live, know this – in the ocean of life the Isles of Blessedness are smiling, and the sunny shore of your ideal awaits your coming. Keep your hand firmly upon the helm of thought. In the bark of your soul reclines the commanding Master; He does but sleep; wake Him. Self-control is strength. Right thought is mastery. Calmness is power. Say unto your heart, 'Peace, be still!'

(Allen 1992)

There is nothing more important in this life than tranquility and serenity. It is for this reason that Paul in 1 Timothy 2:2 asks us to pray 'for kings and all who are in high positions' (NRSV). It does not matter how much wealth a person has. It does not matter how much power or status. It does not matter how much intelligence or education. The success of our life is brought about by the amount of Godly serenity we possess and our ability to see the emerging horizon where heaven and earth touch. The need for serenity and its relationship to will and the discovering of our existential horizon is beautifully expressed in Reinhold Niebuhr's serenity prayer: 'God grant me the serenity to accept the things I cannot change, the courage to change the things that I can and the wisdom to know the difference.'

8

Existential Hope, Mood and Will

We have heard such expressions as, 'He has a lot of energy!' 'I don't know where he gets his energy!' 'I wish I had his energy!' 'I just don't have the energy I used to have!' I suggest these expressions are metaphors that we use to express the idea of mental energy. When we talk about mental energy, we talk like this mental energy is a real moving power like physical energy. It is as if we have a source of energy in a container. It seems we are inclined to think of our inner power as a container.

The expression 'mental energy' is not really about having a container of something like a physical, driving force of energy. Mental energy is about the ideas, feelings, emotions, and beliefs that motivate us to action. When we are talking about mental energy, we are really talking about willpower. Instead of saying, 'Where does he get his energy?' it is more accurate to say, 'Where does he get his willpower?' C.R. Snyder defines willpower as, 'The driving force in hopeful thinking. It is the sense of mental energy that over time helps to propel the person.' According to Snyder, willpower is ignited when we are able to 'clearly understand and represent a goal in our minds.' The major issue, from a Snyder perspective, is the ability to clearly understand and represent a goal in our minds. In other words, we must have a clear understanding and representation of our goals before we are propelled into action.

Willpower depends on our ability to clearly understand and represent our goals. It depends on something that must happen in our mind, namely something that takes place because we are able to organize our ideas, emotions, feeling and beliefs. This combination of inner mental operations allows us to exercise our will based on our mind states. It is an expression taken from the approach of Buddhist psychology, which has a better grasp of mind states than Western psychology. Buddhist psychology is grounded on the practice of mindfully examining our inner ideas, thoughts, emotions and feelings as they shape our moods. Buddhist psychology does not hold that ideas, thoughts, emotions and feelings can be examined separately; rather, they always exist as a hybrid mind state.

Perhaps the most outstanding figure in modern philosophy is Martin Heidegger who takes a view that our human nature is shaped primarily by moods. I believe he holds to a position somewhat similar to Buddhist psychology. Our moods are a combination of ideas, thoughts, emotions and feelings. We have heard the expression, 'Well, what kind of a mood are you in?' We ask people if they are in a good or bad mood. On occasions, we may say to someone, 'I'm in a good (or bad) mood today.' When I state, 'I'm in a good (or bad) mood,' it means that I am presently feeling a particular sense of existence. I am present with my mind, body and soul existing in a mood (see Heidegger 1962).

Human beings are both emotional and rational beings. Unfortunately, when we think about exercising our will, we are inclined to believe that willpower comes about as an execution of the rational mind. For example, a person decides to lose weight. The person has come to a point of decision-making, when their inner voice says, 'I have to lose this weight. It does not make sense carrying this weight. I want to look and feel better.' The person has made a resolve and designs a plan of action that he/she will execute to lose the weight. It is a decision and the person resolves to carry it out.

The problem is that willpower does not depend entirely on exercising the rational mind. For example, people say, 'I am just going to make up my mind; you know, get my head around it and diet.' The decision to exercise the will and diet is never just a rational decision because we are creatures of moods. In other words, willpower is affected by our moods. Our moods are shaped by the combination of our emotions and thoughts which shape our feelings. A mood is really the same as the state of feelings that exist in our conscious and unconscious mind.

9

Will Energy and Feelings

The moods control the energy of the will. It is not our thoughts that move us, nor is it our emotions. As stated previously, the energy of the mind-body organism is feelings. Neuroscientific research into the nature of the relationship of the mind-body and the functioning of human decision-making processes argues that decision-making, for the greater part, is controlled by our feelings. Antonio Damasio describes the situation in *Looking for Spinoza: Joy, Sorrow and the Feeling Brain*:

> Elucidating the neurobiology of feelings and their antecedent emotions contributes to our views on the mind-body problem, a problem central to understanding who we are. Emotion and related reactions are aligned with the feelings with the mind. The investigation of how thoughts trigger emotions and how bodily emotions become the kind of thoughts we call feelings provides a privileged view into mind and body, the overtly disparate manifestations of a single and seamlessly interwoven organism.
> (Damasio 2003)

Damasio's fundamental principle is that thoughts trigger our emotions and emotions trigger our thoughts. The constant dynamics of thoughts and emotions puts us in a continuous state of being energized by our feelings. A basic distinction of Damasio on the difference between emotions and feelings is helpful in the understanding of emotions as it relates to will energy:

> Emotions are actions or movements, many of them public, visible to others as they occur in the face, in the voice, in

specific behaviors ... Feelings, on the other hand, are always hidden, like all mental images necessarily are, unseen to anyone other than the rightful owner, the most private property of the organism in whose brain they occur. Emotions play out in the theater of the body. Feelings play out in the theater of the mind.

(Damasio 2003)

Willpower, therefore, is a feeling, an urge, an idea and an action. If I decide to lose weight, I always have a driving feeling first. A person may have a thought about losing weight, but the thought has really come from some feeling or feelings. The Damasio law of living is true; we live primarily by feelings. Our life, desires, goals, hopes and acts of will are shaped by our feelings. We live with a continual drama being acted out in our mind and body, and at any given moment we are happy, excited, jolly, sad, stressed, anxious, thrilled, ambivalent, angry, lonely, cautious, frustrated, in love, peaceful, great, unsure, etc. We are driven in the drama of the mind and body by a cast of feelings.

We are really never in a state of just having a feeling; we have feelings. We exist throughout the day in multiple and sometimes conflicting feelings. For example, we can be happy about our job, thrilled about a coming vacation, anxious about paying for the vacation, and at the same time we are angry with our teenage daughter. It is this play of feelings that are lived in the mind and body that sets our moods. If a person says, 'I am in a bad mood today' or 'I'm in a good mood,' it is because there are, as a rule, a number of feelings occurring. It is the complexity and interaction of feelings that shape our moodiness.

In turn, our character is formed by our moods; we make statements like, 'She is always in a good mood,' 'He is in a bad mood today,' 'Oh, you never know what mood they will be in when you meet them.' We refer to someone as being a moody type person, but, in point of fact, everyone is a moody type person.

10

Moods, Hybrid Feelings and the Will

Our low to high levels of will energy depend on our moods. Just to oversimplify, I divide our mood states into a mood of acceptance or a mood of impedance. A mood of acceptance means that a person is in a good and pleasant mood. A person is willing to accept life and carry out their goals and responsibilities somewhat confidently; the opposite is when a person is in a mood of impedance with a low energy level. A person in a state of impedance has difficulty accepting life. A mood of impedance person has an extremely difficult time accepting life on life's terms.

Usually, we are asked, 'How do you feel today?' or 'How are you doing?' With these types of questions, we are really being asked about what type of mood we are embracing in our mind and body. Seldom do we ask a person about their mood; we do not ask, 'Hey, what kind of a mood are you in today?' There are occasions when we realize that there is something really eating at a person, and we state, 'Gee, you're in a bad mood today. What's wrong?'

Our moods are shaped by our thoughts and feelings; it is the feelings that most predominate in shaping the thoughts. Recent research in neuroscience seems to establish that our feelings almost come in nanoseconds before our thoughts. During the course of a day, a month or a lifetime, we experience multiple emotions.

We also experience the constant combination of feelings, e.g. we can feel happy about our job, but frustrated about our marriage. We can be excited about a coming vacation, but stressed about how we will pay for it. Our feelings seem to rub against one another. We do not just go through life with an overall feeling; rather our feelings are a hybrid. That is, they are always feeding on each other and cross breeding. It is this process of the continuous cross-breeding of our feelings that put us into our moods that shapes our behavior, decision-making and willpower.

It is our moods that shape our will and life goals. It is our moods that define our life choices and existential possibilities. I would suggest that the way we are known by other people more than anything else is for our moods. It was the philosopher Heidegger who taught that our entire relationship with others, life and the world is shaped by our moods. Heidegger made an extremely clear and critical distinction between the nature of emotions and moods. Emotions are concerned about particular things. I am angry about something or with someone. But I am in an irritable mood. Often we are in a certain mood, but we cannot identify any particular person or event. Moods are directed at life and our participation with the world (Inwood 1997).

Our emotions are constantly stimulated by the events and happenings of life. If we are awake or asleep, the emotional brain is always actively feeling its way through life. The material brain is a result of our evolutionary process of adaptation and survival in our environment. The emotions are critical to this survival because they are a continuous feedback system. The evolutionary psychology of Robert Plutchik refers to the brain as an instrument of accepting one's environment or being threatened by the environment.

Plutchik describes people as being in a state of either emotional willingness or unwillingness. Emotions of acceptance are anticipation, joy, trust and fear, and the emotions of unwillingness are anger, disgust, sadness and surprise. As defined above, emotions are seen as the hardware of the brain that has resulted from humankind's evolutionary/biological adaptation to the environment. As stated, it is necessary to make a distinction between emotions and feelings. The emotions are the raw microevolutionary hardware of the brain. When the mind begins to respond to emotions, the drama of the mind is driven by feelings; the feelings result in a continuous conscious and subconscious charge of feelings. It is the various feelings and thoughts of the hybrid mind that set our moods. Using Plutchik's emotions classification, we are able to refer to a person as being in a mood of either acceptance or unwillingness towards life. This classification is extremely important in the understanding of the exercise of the will, because the exercise of will is much more than a mere choice and decision. Our will is primarily an inner dialogue of the unconscious feeling mind comprised of the feeling voices of willingness and unwillingness.

11

Existential Willingness and Unwillingness

Every human being has two basic moods that define their existence, i.e. willingness or unwillingness. What we call willpower is determined by these two moods of willingness or unwillingness. When we face an issue in life that requires a serious and sustained effort of our will, it depends fundamentally on our mood. When we interact, on any given day or moment, why and how we interact depends on whether we are in a mood of willingness or unwillingness. Our subjective response to people and situations depends on whether we have a positive mood of willingness or a negative mood. Even more important, successful exercising of our will is completely dependent on the state of our willingness and/or unwillingness moods. The reality of the dialectical tension in our life of willingness and unwillingness describes the basic existential metaphysical truth of all humanity. The human condition is always the fundamental option of being (willingness) or non-being (unwillingness).

Every one of us awakes each day to face the basic existential challenge to our will. It is the issue of whether we are willing or unwilling to face the challenge of discovering the nature of our authentic self and begin the courageous movement of the will to become. In other words, will we accept or reject the day? In a mood of acceptance, we approach the events of the day and the exercise of will filled with the energy of willingness. We begin to move through each day with the energy of optimistic interest, serenity, acceptance, trust and rational fear. It is noted that fear is a necessary emotion inherited from our genetic past. A will existing in a willingness state senses the threats and dangers of life only as guides to achieving life's goals. If we exist in a mood of unwillingness then life is filled with feelings of anger, annoyance, contempt, distraction, grief etc. It is when we are in the existential mood of unwillingness that the will comes into a brooding range of no interest in life to neutrality at best.

Our will is always wrapped by this hybrid of feelings. It is in the exercising of will that life begins to take meaning. What is the basic nature of humanity? What is the fundamental and universal truth that explains the nature of humanity? What is the basic metaphysical truth of the universe? An existentialist perspective of life rests on the assumption that we have a will. The most vital description of being human is that we are in the continuous process of making our future based on our decisions.

From the perspective of a Christian existentialism, we live a joyful, free and happy life to the extent that we have hope. Living a life of hope is at the heart of mystical awareness. For example, the Buddha looks within to answer the question of suffering and pain in his life. As he meditates and enters into enlightenment, he finds that hope is about living a life of loving compassion. The Buddha comes to his Original Mind, where he learns that the energy of life is giving and receiving loving compassion. The Buddha discovers the hope of his future, i.e. a life of loving compassion; it is an existential horizon.

This existential hope is something much stronger than being positive and having an optimistic view of life. It is the energy that arises from the soul; it is a true spiritual and practical hope. It is the hope of spiritual teachers, and it is the foundation of a positive psychology and philosophy: 'Hope differs fundamentally, however, from the learned optimism perspective. Hope is more than distancing oneself from and delimiting the impact of failures; hope is the essential process of linking oneself to potential success' (Snyder 1994, 18).

Hope is an act of the will. We have only the hope of being a self-actualized person, but we must exercise the will in order to continuously move towards our true and complete self. I am presenting a view much different from the popular and simplistic concept of brain-based willpower. In terms of Christian existentialism the true will exists in the soul. We have lower levels of will that allow us to achieve the lesser decisions and goals of life. However, to define and move to our existential horizons, we must calmly and confidently enter into the energy of the soul.

12

The Existential Soul

What is this soul where we touch into the nature of our true self? We have a soul because we are able to come to awareness that we are spiritual beings. The way to a life of existential hope is when we realize that we are spiritual beings with a body, rather than a body with a spirit. As soon as a person begins to examine the nature of spirituality and begins to practice living a spiritual life, there is a growing awareness of being a spiritual being. We express this stirring of the soul even in a skeptic and cynical postmodern culture with words like, 'Well, you know there just has to be some force that explains this life.'

In order to understand how to enter into the soul where we discover the true will, we must have an existential awareness of the Spirit. The best dynamic teaching on the nature of the Spirit I have found is in *The Science of Mind: A Philosophy, A Faith, A Way of Life* by Ernest Holmes:

> God, within Whom all spirits exist. The Self Knowing One. The Conscious Universe. The Absolute. Spirit in man is that part of him which enables him to know himself. That which he really is. We do not see the spirit of man any more than we see the Spirit of God. We see what man does; but we do not see the doer. We treat of Spirit as the Active and the only self-Conscious principle Spirit as the First Cause or God; the Universal I Am. The Spirit is self-Propelling. It is All; It is self-existent and has all life within Itself. It is the Word and the Word is volition. It is Will because It chooses, and nothing different from Itself. Spirit is the Father Mother God because It is the Principle Unity back of all things. Spirit is all Life, Truth, Love, Being, Cause AND Effect, and is the only Power

in the universe that knows Itself.

(Holmes 1997)

I remember a lady saying to me, 'Father, my life was filled with addiction and pain until one day I became aware that I am a spiritual being in a material body.' In this statement, we hear the marvelous and mysterious voice of the inner soul coming to us in the thought and feeling that we are a spiritual being which comes from our soul. It is the soul where we discover our superconscious awareness of the divinity and the unity of God's world in love.

As Holmes states, in our soul we find the power to activate the Spirit by word and will. It is the same as the ancient teachings of Christian mystics and scholars that in the soul we discover the two essential faculties of the soul, i.e. mind and will. No one has ever seen the mind or Spirit, but from the awareness of the existential soul we know that Spirit, Mind and Divine Will exists.

As we explore deeper and deeper into our soul in prayer and meditation, we come to know that there is no such thing as your mind and my mind, his mind, her mind and God's mind. There is just mind, in which we live, move and have our being. Mind is both conscious and subconscious or subjective (Holmes 1997, 612). The soul's faculty of will brings to execution the urges, thoughts and impulses of the Spirit. With the discovery that in the soul is only God's mind, we discover that our will and God's will is one and the same.

What is it that blocks us from experiencing and knowing the energy of our soul? It is our moods of unwillingness! When we are overtaken by moods of unwillingness, we withdraw from life. When we withdraw from life, there is no mystery to pursue; there are no exciting existential horizons. When we live in unwillingness, life becomes a superficial play of anger, annoyance, loathing, boredom, remorse, grief, sadness, disapproval, distraction, terror and, most of all, depression and anxiety.

The issue of willingness or unwillingness is the fundamental existential option that human beings must exercise in approaching life. It is similar to Snyder's view in *The Psychology of Hope*:

> Yet another characteristic that should go along with hope is positive affectivity. Positive affectivity is a mental state characterized by full concentration, engagement, and high energy. It is a way of thinking in which our minds are interested, excited, strong, enthusiastic, proud, alert, inspired, determined, attentive and active ... the flip side of positive affectivity is a negative affectivity, a general state of subjective distress including nervousness, contempt, anger, fear and guilt.
>
> (Snyder 1994)

The willingness/unwillingness existential option is a concept with a deeper meaning than positive or negative thinking. It is an existential option existing deeply in the body, mind and soul of a person. The opting for a life of willingness is a basic spiritual and philosophical choice that affects every aspect of life and particularly affects the establishing of a person's soul based on their authentic existential horizon.

We are touching upon the existential issue of anxiety, despair and angst as part and parcel of the human condition. In a Christian existentialism, it is the ability to live in spiritual hope and love that is the most satisfying existential option. The real threat to a life that is happy, joyous and free is when we not only live an existence of unwillingness, but also begin to brood in our primary mood of unwillingness. When we enter into a state of brooding, unwillingness becomes a deep-seated state of conscious feeling. As a matter of fact, it becomes the driving mood that becomes the belief system that drives our existence.

13

Zen, the Soul and Willingness

If we are to have a profound and pragmatic spirituality, we must allow the soul to disclose our existential horizon. Christian existential spirituality is always a pursuit in hope in a world that is easily drawn into a culture of unwillingness. Paraphrasing the philosopher Herbert Spencer, it is a culture of contempt (unwillingness) prior to investigation (willingness).

A powerful figure of Positive Psychology, C.R. Snyder writes, 'A new view of hope is needed as we enter the twenty-first century. My belief is that hope is a specific way of thinking about oneself rather than some nebulous, immeasurable philosophical notion.' A Christian Zen is decidedly about the method and practice of developing a specific way of hopeful thinking: 'I press on toward the goal for the prize of the upward call of God in Christ Jesus. Let those of us who are mature be thus minded ... God will reveal that also to you. Only let us hold true to what we have attained' (Philippians 3:14–16 NRSV). This passage from Philippians is a clear expression of a Christian existentialism of hope, and our hope is based on Christ-like mindfulness.

Christian Zen is a willingness practice that allows us to enter the energy of the inner Christ. In a sense, Zen is a tool for living in a mood of willingness, and it is by living in willingness that we are able to become. The practice of Zen is a pragmatic way of living. Often, we hear the criticism of institutional religion that it is not relevant today. Most of Western religion seems based on claims of truth among various Catholic and Protestant traditions. Christian Zen, on the other hand, is concerned only with the spiritual practice of entering into a willingness to bring Christ into the ordinary events of our life. Christian Zen is the practice of finding the ordinary in the extraordinary of life and living in the energy of an existential horizon. Hal French in an extraordinary work, *Zen and the Art of Anything*, defines Zen as a method even independent of any particular expression of Buddhism. He describes Zen as a way of the ordinary becoming the extraordinary:

> As R.H. Blyth reminds us, 'When the sacred really equals the profane, we have Zen.' That means that we will focus here on the tasks that each of us performs, daily (or regularly, or routinely), but so very seldom does in a mindful, reflective way: breathing and speaking, waking and sleeping, moving and staying, eating and drinking, playing and working, caring and loving, thriving and striving, These are birth to death life cycle activities in which we all engage ... I once had a student, David, who was taking an independent study in Sanskrit with me while he was also enrolled in structured courses in Greek, Hebrew, Latin, Arabic, and Chinese. Impressive! I thought, of course, that he was aspiring to become a consummate classical linguist, but his vocational ambition was to become a house painter. He simply wanted to have some facility for the rest of his life whatever he did vocationally, to study the great religious traditions in their original languages. His was the purest liberal arts ideal I've ever encountered. In fact, he didn't become a house painter, but a plumber, and a good one. A personal reference: he's often worked for me! Maybe he picked up naturally, with reference to classical languages, the concluding insight of Marian Mountain's book *The Zen Environment*, when she observed simply, 'Zen is a plumber's helper. It is the most mundane tool for the most practical of tasks.'
>
> (French 1999)

When the sacred touches the profane, it is when we hit upon our existential horizon. As we enter into this horizon, we touch the energy of our soul. The above story of David is about a person who has found the energy of his soul and his existential horizon. We are not all called to positions of high leadership, powerful influence in the arts, politics, education, religion, business, etc. Yet, as we see with David, the existential horizon is found in the ordinary events of life.

Zen Buddhism and Christian Zen are expressions of soul mysticism where the idea of the existence of God is, in any expressible form, absent. Soul is numinous and hidden. In soul mysticism, the Zen Buddhist enters into the Original Mind, and in Christian Zen we enter into the inner Christ. In Zen Buddhism and Christian Zen, the soul is entered when it is released from everything it is not. In Zen, the ego self and the material world are obliterated until the authentic spiritual self and the existential horizon are disclosed. It is in the experience of no-thing that we find everything.

14

Zen and the Loyalty of the Soul

Josiah Royce wrote:

Man needs no miracles to show him the supernatural and the superhuman. You need no signs and wonders, and no psychical research, to prove that the unity of the spirit is a fact in the world. Common sense tacitly presupposes the reality of the unity of the spirit. Science studies the ways in which its life is expressed in the laws which govern the order of experience. Reason gives us insight into its real being. Loyalty serves, and repents not of the service. Salvation means our positive harmony with loyalty's purpose and with its manifestations.

This American philosopher, in his work *The Sources of Religious Insight*, puts forth a metaphysics grounded on an intellectual and spiritual drive of loyalty to a higher cause. The drive for purpose in life is never just an individual existential pursuit because the drive for purpose always involves the need for a community experience of meaning. The pursuit of a higher ideal cause, the feeling of salvation that comes with being part of a community sustained and nurtured in a higher ideal experience, Royce sees as the essence of a religious community.

From this perspective, he suggests:

The higher religions of mankind's religions such as Buddhism and Christianity have had in common this notable feature, namely, that they have been concerned with the problem of Salvation of Man. This is sometimes expressed by saying that they are redemptive religions – religions interested in freeing mankind from some vast and universal burden, of imperfection, of unreasonableness, of evil, of misery, of fate, of unworthiness, or of sin.

It is interesting when I talk about spiritual matters with friends from Alcoholics Anonymous who make a clear distinction between the spirituality of a 12-step program and traditional religion. As we continue in the dialogue, I soon realize that their description of their 12-step spirituality fits into Royce's description of religion. There is a revelation of some type in a person that there is a power greater than the self-reliance and self-will. Indeed, the person has been led to this revelation because of the inability of their will to overcome unbearable inner demons.

Royce holds that it is the realization of a higher ideal that allows the individual to escape the bondage of a feeble will and self-identity:

First, his Ideal, that is, the standard in terms of how he estimates the sense and value of his own personal life; secondly his need of salvation, that is, the degree to which he falls short of attaining his ideal and is sundered from it by evil fortune, or by his own paralysis of will or by his inward baseness; thirdly, the presence or the coming or the longing for, or the communion with something which comes to view as the power that may save him from his need, or as the light that may dispel the darkness or as the truth that shows him the way out, or as the great companion who helps him in a word as his Deliverer. The Ideal, the Need, the Deliverer – these are the three objects which the individual experience, as a source religious insight, has always undertaken to reveal.

I thought of Royce's metaphysics of loyalty to the Ideal, when I was on a spiritual retreat with Christians led by an American Zen

Buddhist monk. The monk was teaching us, throughout the day, the practice of Zazen and the principles and methods of the Zen Buddhist Soto tradition. In the evening, we had wonderful dialogue sessions with the monk from the leading Zen temple in the United States. One evening, a lady addressed a simple straightforward question to the Zen teacher: 'What caused you to become interested in Zen Buddhism?'

The monk explained that when he was a young man he had had a drug problem. He had even spent a short time in prison. After he had been released, he saw himself as completely demoralized like most alcoholics and addicts in the advanced stages of their addiction. In terms of an existential option, he was demoralized because of a paralysis of will. His only hope, therefore, was to enter into a state of willingness in order to find a power (an ideal) greater than his own self-will.

The monk had to face the existential option of willingness or unwillingness in order to live as a happy, joyous and free person. If so, he must discover the energy of his soul by entering into a mindset of willingness. The monk became aware that his existential being was in need of a higher ideal. He was in need of a salvific power that would save him from the paralysis of his will. Third, he required a light that would save him from his darkness and the pain of suffering – a Deliverer, the Buddha.

We find the same three objectives in the teaching of the 12 steps of Alcoholics Anonymous:

1 We admitted we were powerless over alcohol – that our lives had become unmanageable.
2 We came to believe that a Power greater than ourselves could restore us to sanity.
3 We made a decision to turn our will and our lives over to the care of God as we understood Him.

Royce was also adamant on the social and community aspect of religion as necessary for the disclosure of the existential self. As a matter of fact, from a Roycian perspective we are only able to discover our existential core by means of self-interpretation:

> But we have found that we could not decide how the Christian doctrine of life is related to the real world without defining what we mean by community. A community, as we have seen, depends for its very constitution upon the way in which each of its members interprets himself and his life. For the rest, nobody's self is either a mere datum or an abstract conception. A self is a life whose unity and connectedness depend upon some sort of interpretation of plans, of memories, of hopes and deeds ... If, then, there are communities, there are many selves who, despite their variety, so interpret their lives that all these lives, taken together. Were there, then, no interpretations in the world, there would be neither selves nor communities.
>
> (Royce, *The Problem of Christianity*, General Books, reprint 2010, 30)

Zen Buddhism is often portrayed as a mostly individualistic method of meditation and approach to spirituality. Although Buddhism has monasteries and monks, in the popular pursuit it is seen as a way for a person to supplement an individual spiritual journey. It is seen as an addition to an individual existential journey. Yet, Buddhism in its core beliefs is essentially constructed on the belief in a brotherhood and sisterhood of practitioners:

1 I take refuge in the Buddha, i.e. the true awakened state. It is the ideal pursuit to disclose the Buddha nature.
2 I take refuge in the Dharma, i.e. the belief in the basic teachings of the Buddha of the Original Mind and the escape from pain and suffering in living a life of loving

compassion.

3 I take refuge in the Sangha, i.e. the need for the sustaining community of practitioners and the interpretation and application of the Buddha's teachings.

Christian Zen holds to the Pauline epistles' teaching on the nature of an interpretative community in Philippians:

> If you have any encouragement from being united with Christ, if any comfort from his love, if any fellowship with the Spirit, if any tenderness and compassion, then make my joy complete by being likeminded, having the same love, being one in spirit and purpose. Do nothing out of selfish ambition or vain conceit, but in humility consider others better than yourselves. Each of you should look not only to your own interests ...
>
> (Philippians 2:1–4 NIV)

The practice of Christian Zen as a method of prayer and existential affirmation adheres primarily to the teachings of the gospel, especially in terms of Christianity being a process which is similar to Buddhism; the spirituality is grounded on three basic beliefs as they are disclosed in John 14:2–4:

> 'I am going there to prepare a place for you. And if I go and prepare a place for you, I will come back and take you to be with me that you also may be where I am. You know the way to the place where I am going.'
>
> Thomas said to him, 'Lord, we don't know where you are going, so how can we know the way?'
>
> Jesus answered, 'I am the way and the truth and the life.'
> (NIV)

In this passage, Jesus explains his teaching with the proclamation, 'I am the way.' Jesus is talking about a way that calls for a loyal response from his followers. Jesus is not proclaiming metaphysics or a systematic theology. It is a way of living a spiritual existence: 'I tell you the truth, anyone who has faith in me will do what I have been doing' (John 14:12 NIV).

Christian Zen is concerned with the spiritual process of disclosing the inner Christ. In a sense, the practitioner of Christian Zen could easily restate the three Buddhist core teachings as:

1 I take refuge in the Christ.
2 I take refuge that Christ is the way, the truth and the life.
3 I take refuge in the Christian community.

15

Zen and the Christian Samurai

The relationship between the way of the Christian life and the way of the samurai is a concept taken from the work of Paul Nowak. It is in the way of the samurai that we have a spiritual process similar to the practice of Christian Zen:

> As Christians, our Way is Jesus Christ – the Way, the Truth, the Life. Just because we hear of something that rings true in the way of the samurai does not mean the way of Jesus and the way of the samurai are the same; however, as we grow in our faith and understanding of the Jesus Way, we can begin to enrich our understanding of how we ought to live our lives from examples beyond His teachings – even from followers of the philosophies, such as the samurai.
>
> (Nowak 2005)

Christian Zen is not a discipline that practices Zazen (meditation) to achieve satori (enlightenment). Christian Zen is a method of prayer, meditation and loyal service to the teachings of Jesus and disclosing of the inner Christ in a life of loving service to others, i.e. an ethics of loving compassion. 'Samurai' means to serve others, to be loyal and obedient to the master. A samurai spent his life in the practice of service and loyalty to the master. It is the samurai's singleness of purpose that calls him to a high-level consciousness of duty and the dedication of the will to the way of the warrior. This extreme focus calls for the samurai warrior to engage in the continuous process of clearing the mind to the ethics of the samurai and the will to exercise the ethical values:

If one were to say in a word what the condition of being a samurai is, its basis lies first in seriously devoting one's body and soul to his master. And if one is asked what to go do beyond this, it would be to fit oneself inwardly with intelligence, humanity and courage ... Intelligence is nothing more than discussing with others. Limitless wisdom comes from this. Humanity is something done for the sake of others, simply comparing oneself with them and putting them in the fore. Courage is gritting one's teeth; it is simply doing that and pushing ahead, paying no attention to the circumstances. If you think it over, being a retainer (servant) is simple.

(From the Hagakure, Book 2)

In this passage, we encounter a religious and ethical tradition in the Roycian sense of loyalty and learning and nurturing of the ethical way from a life spent in a community of obedience and loyalty.

By means of such a spiritual way, the warrior is dedicated to a life of spiritual, moral and physical courage. It requires finding the will for such a path in the deep core of the existential being. In turn, the life of the samurai becomes the ever present existential horizon: 'It is simply doing that and pushing ahead.' It is the call to loyalty that shapes the spiritual consciousness of the samurai and his disciplined spirituality of loyalty:

There is surely nothing other than the single purpose of the present moment. A man's whole life is a succession of moment after moment, there will be nothing else to do, nothing else to pursue, but living true to the single purpose of the moment.

Everyone lets the present moment slip by, and then looks for it as though he thought it was somewhere else. No one seems to have noticed this fact. But grasping this firmly, one must pile experience upon experience. And once one has come to the understanding he will be a different person from that point on, though he may not always bear it in mind. When one understands this settling into single mindedness, his affairs will thin out. Loyalty is also contained in single mindedness.

(Hagakure, Book 2)

Martin Heidegger, in his short work *Discourse on Thinking*, draws attention to the reality that more and more thinking in a technological age is instrumental and operative. It is concerned with scientific/technological improvement. It is a world no longer concerned with ultimate causation as much as the most pragmatic scientific causal explanation of the world.

> Its peculiarity consists in the fact that whenever we plan, research, and organize, we always reckon with conditions that are given. We take them into account with the calculated intention of their specific purposes. Thus we can count the definite results. This calculation is the mark of all thinking that plans and investigates. Such thinking remains calculation even if it neither works with numbers nor uses an adding machine or computer. Calculative thinking computes. It computes ever new, ever more promising computers.

Heidegger then describes two kinds of thinking, each justified and needed in its own way: calculative thinking and meditative thinking (Heidegger, 1966).

Heidegger describes meditative thinking as 'what we have in mind when we say that contemporary man is in flight from thinking.' This meditative thinking is when we float above reality; it is a thinking that is above the reach of ordinary understanding. Most importantly, meditative thinking is open to every human being. The practice of meditative thinking is rather similar to the Buddhist concept of mindful and the samurai practice of 'single mindedness.' In Heidegger's meditative thinking, 'we dwell on what lies close, and meditate on what is closest; upon that which concerns us, each one of us, here and now; here on this patch of home ground; now in the present hour of history.' The existential purpose of meditative thinking is that we silence the voices of the calculative ego in order to touch the inner Christ and our existential horizon that Heidegger refers to as 'here on this patch of home ground.'

16

Three Pillars of Christian Zen

First, Western Christianity since the time of Augustine has seen man as being basically evil according to Augustine's concept of original sin. However, modern and enlightened biblical scholarship teaches that there is really no such concept in scripture. It was a teaching of Augustine wrongly adopted by the early church. Zen is much closer than Augustine to Jesus' authentic teaching about the nature of man. In Jesus' teaching, as in all Buddhism, man is basically a loving and compassionate being. Buddhism argues that every human being desires to be happy, but deep and lasting happiness is found only by extending compassion to those who suffer. We have exactly the same basic teaching in Jesus' teaching on the beatitudes.

If it is natural to want happiness, then it is also natural that we are made by God as fundamentally compassionate people. We are held back from our compassionate nature, according to Buddhist teachings, by our destructive emotions. These dark emotions of greed, anger and confusion are similar to the gospel teaching of sin and demonic voices in our unconscious mind. The major issue in Zen, as in Christian spirituality, is: How do we overcome the destructive, demonic and unwillingness voices of the unconscious mind? The answer is by means of meditation because meditation allows us to become balanced and calm so that our higher mind will appear and guide us to true happiness.

Second, like Christianity, if we want to find happiness, we can never find it by looking outside ourselves. We must find happiness only by means of the inner higher mind. We find a very similar teaching of the higher mind in Paul's epistle to the Philippians:

If you have any encouragement from being united with Christ, if any comfort from his love, if any fellowship with the Spirit, if any tenderness and compassion, then make my joy complete by being likeminded, having the same love, being one in the spirit and purpose. Do nothing out of selfish ambition or vain conceit, but in humility consider others better than you. Each of you should not look only to your own interests, but also to the interests of others.

(Philippians 2:1–4 NIV)

The higher mind of Zen or putting on the mind of Philippians comes about when we meditate and escape the lower destructive mind. The higher mind of Christ is like the moon that is hidden by clouds of darkness, but in prayer and meditation it slowly becomes a bright, full moon. It is when we experience this higher mind that we are moved to acts of 'tenderness and compassion.' In traditional Christian meditation we expect to hear in our prayers and meditation the voice of God. It is called in Western theology the Vox Dei.

Third, we expect from God clear thoughts and feelings to come out of the meditations of our hearts. It is as we read in Psalm 99:7: 'He spoke to them from the pillar of cloud; they kept his statutes and the decrees he gave them' (NIV). Christian Zen meditation is about allowing the cloud to clear so we can gradually hear the message from God. Often, when Christians hear this message they are moved to write the message down and play with it for days. 'In Zen Buddhism, having left the clouded mind, the disciple is moved by impulses from the higher mind. When we enter into calmness and serenity of our higher mind, creative impulses come to our conscious mind.'

The gospel teaches the importance of the 'seed' in living a spiritual life. For example, 'Jesus put before them another parable: The kingdom of heaven is like a mustard seed that someone took and sowed in his field; it is the smallest of all the seeds, but when it has grown it is the greatest of shrubs and becomes a tree, so that the birds of the air come and make nests in its branches' (Matthew 13:31–32 NRSV).When we experience in meditation the love of Jesus, we are moved to having creative impulses. A creative impulse is about how we share in creating God's kingdom on earth with the disclosure of our existential horizon.

Let us take an example of a Christian man who is unhappy with his job. He is just doing it, but he does not feel that his talents are really being used. Before he begins to search around for another job, he decides to put on the mind of Christ, i.e. his higher mind. He does not get strategic at the outset because he wants the creative impulse before he makes any decision. He decides to enter into heavy meditation for two weeks, but during the meditation a creative impulse hits him throughout the day: 'Hey, maybe God wants me to stay where I am and have a change of attitude!' After experiencing this creative impulse, he returns to his job with a new attitude, and he becomes a better and happier employee. At the same time, the creative impulse has moved him to do more volunteer work and extend compassion to those who suffer. He plants the seed in the field (his mind), and he becomes a more dynamic person who brings happiness to others. He has grown and becomes 'the greatest of shrubs and becomes a tree so that the birds of the air come and make nests in the branches of his personality.'

17

The Daily Exercise of Christian Zen

When I do a workshop or lecture on Christian meditation and Zen, the topic seems to arouse an immediate caution if not skepticism. There is the unwarranted belief that meditation belongs to monks and nuns living either as Christian or Buddhist monastics. I stress that I am not a monastic; I am a pastor of a Christian community in the evolving process of adapting to a postmodern culture. It is well beyond the scope and intention of this paper to explain the nature of postmodernism.

An easy way to describe postmodernism is to state that we live in an information society where we are continuously bombarded with information. Postmodern culture is dedicated to the transmission of information, and this transmission of information is used in ever ongoing ways to nourish our calculative thinking. In the information culture, we are driven by the most efficient use of information, and are consequently obsessed with calculative cost/benefit analysis.

In an information culture, without the practice of meditation and meditative thinking, we are in danger of losing our soul. I am attempting in this work to define a lifestyle that allows us to live in the presence of Christ. I am an Episcopal priest and spiritual mentor. I am a Trinitarian. In my spiritual tradition, we pursue the presence of Christ in word, sacrament, prayer, meditation, and spiritual reading for the purpose of bringing Christ's love and healing presence to others. We teach the importance of presence, and it is a spiritual concept of being present similar to the Buddhist teaching on mindfulness.

In Christian Zen, living in Christ mindfulness and presence in every aspect of our life is the same. It is Christ mindfulness and exercise of will that is our energy. Christian Zen is not a synthesis of Christianity and Buddhism. It borrows from Zen concepts and practices that enhance the presence of Christ in our daily life. Christ presence becomes more concrete and action-oriented because our mind and will are in a constant state of Christ mindfulness.

We often hear the discussion today about the difference between religion and meditation. I suggest that the main difference between religion and spirituality is in the experience of time. Somehow, we have developed a belief in Western Christianity that both the acceptance of Jesus and the proper interpretation of scripture put one in a spiritual condition of security in time. We rest secure in the fact that the Christian and the rest of humanity are sinners, but the Christian has accepted Christ. It is the acceptance of Christ as Lord and Savior that allows the person to obtain eternal salvation and live in eschatological time, i.e. awaiting the second coming.

Spirituality, on the other hand, is about entering into the Christ mind on the basis of daily time and living in the now by means of prayer and meditation. It is a continuous daily practice of being spiritually fit on any given day. When we enter into Zen-like meditation, we are expressing that we are moving into an existential state of spiritual awareness. In this state of willingness, we leave the limitations of the ego. It is the ego (the limited self) that finds it more comfortable to exist in states of unwillingness. It is in meditation that we become open to the burning love of the inner Christ which is where the Original Self is disclosed. In Christian Zen existential meditation we learn that:

1 Each mind is unique and must find its distinctive spiritual path.
2 Every mind feels and knows God in a distinctive and existential way.
3 The practice of meditation, even without religious beliefs,

improves physical and emotional health and increases problem-solving skills.

4 Long-term meditation gives us better control of our moods, a courageous acceptance of our authentic self and our plans for a joyous, free and happy life.

5 Long-term meditation generates serenity, peacefulness, social awareness, social skills and Christ-like loving compassion for others.

Christian Zen is a way of living in the world of daily events and is concerned with the issue of meaning and the effort to live in loving compassion with others. Christian Zen is basically a method of centering prayer and meditation. If I could describe this Zen approach to prayer and meditation, it is minimalism. It is not an abstract method of meditation and prayer. It is similar in purpose and practice to *The Cloud of Unknowing* written in 1413 by an unknown author. It is a Dionysian approach to the spiritual life where the plane of the spiritual experience is reached by a way with which the intellect cannot deal. The view of the contemplation found in the Cloud is demanding and action-oriented in that there is no short cut to hidden knowledge or super-sensual experience; rather it demands a keen employment of the will, coupled with self-knowledge, humility and charity. There is no trace of quietism or spiritual limpness, but an insistence on controlled activity and wholeness of experience. 'A man,' it says, 'may not be fully active, but he is in part contemplative; nor yet fully contemplative, as it may be here, but be in part active' (*Cloud of Unknowing*).

It is a spirituality that by means of breathing and using simple words for prayer and meditation is adaptable to today's daily life. If we are to sense the stirring in our heart to experience the energy of our soul, the *Cloud* recommends:

And if thee list have the intent lapped and folden in one word, for thou shouldest have better hold thereupon, take thee but a little word of one syllable: for so it is the better it accordeth than of two, for the shorter it is better it accordeth with the work of the Spirit. And such a word is this word God or this word love. Choose thee whether thou wilt or another; all thee list, which that thee whether thou wilt or another; as thee list, which that thee liketh best of one syllable. And fasten this word to thine heart, so that it never go thence for thing that befalleth.

This word shall be thy shield and thy spear, whether thou ridest on peace or war. With this word, thou shalt smite down all manner of thought under the cloud of forgetting. Insomuch that of any thought press upon thee to ask thee what thou wouldst have, answer him no more words but this one word. And if he proffer thee of his great clergy to expound thee that word and to tell thee the conditions of that word say to him: That thou wilt have it all whole, and not broken nor undone. And if thou wilt hold thee fast on this purpose, be thou sure, he will no while abide. And why? For that thou wilt not let him feed him on such sweet meditations of God touched before.

(Happold 1963)

An existential Christian Zen requires dedicated spiritual exercises for calming and clearing the mind. A basic tenet of an existential view of humanity is that it is the human condition to exist in a natural condition of anxiety. We are not talking here about a clinical state of anxiety; rather it is the ever present question of death and meaning. In the Samurai *Hagakure*, Book 10, it teaches, 'It is said that becoming as a dead man in one's daily living is following the path of sincerity.' As Nowak explains:

Through their view of themselves as already dead, the samurai were able to overcome fear. This did not mean that they were fearless; rather, they accepted that death was inevitable, and embraced the idea of dying in the service of their lord to the degree that they no longer lived for themselves. Fear is imposing, but all fear is an anxious anticipation of loss.

(Nowak 2005)

In the samurai philosophy, they face boldly and continuously the confrontation with the ever present overriding existential mood; it is the sense of loss and non-meaning. The existentialist, like the samurai warrior, faces the issue of death in order to live a life of courage and meaning.

In Christian Zen, the place where we confront death and meaning is by allowing the inner Christ to disclose our existential horizon, i.e. Heidegger's ground where the person finds meaning in this life. However, coming to the core of our being where the inner Christ is disclosed is not achieved by philosophical or theological speculation. It is achieved by entering into an intuitive spiritual state of existence. Human consciousness hopelessly exists in a state of anxiety because the mind dwells on the past with mindsets of success or failure and rushes to the future in an anxiety mood of 'I must do this, time is short, I am losing my health.' The spiritual path is to face our existential condition of loss and anxiety by coming into the present. The human condition is that we live with one foot in the past and one foot in the future and we miss the present.

Living as a Christian existentialist demands that we enter into Zen meditation (Zazen) because in meditation the task is to calm the mind so that we may enter into the Christ within us. It is a way of meditation similar to the Cloud of Unknowing where less is more. It is not discursive thoughts and reflections. It is in silence and focus and the breathing of our sacred words that we calm the mind and experience the love of the inner Christ and our connection in love with all of humanity. These meditation experiences fill us with the energy of loving courage to do the will of God. It is to experience the sense of the energy of divine love where our existential horizon is disclosed. It is the place where that inner Christ places us and calls us to a life of loving loyalty and action.

Part Three

Christian Zen Meditations and Reflections

18

Christian Zen Exercises

Five fundamental practices about the teaching of Christian Zen meditation are the following:

1 Meditation is as natural as sitting and breathing. It is not recommended for Westerners to sit in a difficult lotus, half lotus or Indian style with legs folded. These are natural and comfortable sitting positions in Eastern cultures. It is recommended that a person sit comfortably in a chair with a hard back, sitting with the spine erect, but not rigid. The feet are flat and the shoes are off. It is important to let the tension release from the shoulders and lower back. The key is not to slouch.

2 There are various ways of folding the hands. The fingers can rest on the lap with the fingers gently touching, or relaxed with the palms up. It must be comfortable. In Zen style meditation, the body and hands must feel comfortable with as little stress on the body as possible.

3 In Zen style meditation the breathing is very relaxed and gentle. It is as simple as sitting in a meditative position and as we inhale and exhale we count: we inhale gently from the diaphragm counting one, and exhale on the count of two.

4 In meditation, the mind will always wander because it is the nature of the mind to wander. The biggest mistake is to believe that because a person's mind wanders they cannot meditate. The mind and focus wanders even for people who have meditated for a number of years. It is in the wandering mind that we always find our mystical center and the spiritual authentic self. In meditation, one learns

how to return to the calming center where we again and again focus on our breathing, counting and sacred word or words.

5 There is no such thing as a bad meditation. Everyone must discover their own effective method of meditation. You do not have to live in a monastery. The increase in spiritual, physical and emotional health is possible with a steady daily discipline of 10, 15, or 20 minutes a day in any special, quiet, and calm place.

Meditation I: Christian Zen Disidentification

The concept and practice of Christian Zen is very similar to the teachings of Roberto Assagioli, M.D., on the practice of psychosynthesis. He was an Italian psychiatrist who developed a system of psychological and spiritual transformation.

He used psychosynthesis to help his patients escape from false constructs of their self that prevented them from disclosing their existential self and horizon. When we become identified only with the outward self, identity is based on social roles and beliefs that give us the most gratification. For example, intellectuals identify themselves with their intellects; athletes identify themselves with their bodies, etc.

Psychosynthesis uses a disidentification exercise that takes us inside ourselves and allows us to face our continuous outward-tending identity. It is the purpose of this exercise to start us on the lifetime path of letting go of all forms of false identification.

Method

This exercise gives us a sense of our inner energy that expresses itself when we enter into meditative calmness and quiet the 'monkey brain.'

1 Sit in a relaxed meditative position; some quiet music and the lighting of a candle are useful.

2 Begin to inhale (one) and exhale (two), slowly counting 1, 2, ...

3 Read: 'I have a body, but I am not my body.'

4 My body has various physical conditions, e.g. sick, healthy, tired, rested, etc. It is always changing, but it is not my inner core, my existential horizon.

5 'I have feelings, but I am not my feelings.'

6 My feelings change constantly from moods of willingness to unwillingness, but they are not my existential horizon. My feelings and moods are not the true self.

7 'I have an intellect, but I am not my intellect.'

8 My intellect looks at the world and organizes plans and sees the world in categories and parts. My thoughts and ideas change. The intellect is always interpreting and reinterpreting my life, but my life is at the core of my being, in my soul and in my existential horizon.

9 I am a center of pure awareness. It is in the practice of calm silence and breathing the mantra 'I am' that the energy of the inner true existential self is experienced.

10 Now begin to breathe the mantra 'I am' for 5, 10, 15 minutes.

In this meditation we detach from the flood of trivial impressions that fill our mind. We rest in calmness, and breathe. We do not fight the noise running through our mind and body. We let it come and go, and we return to the breathing. When we stop fighting the noise, we find the quiet space within us. The challenge is not to stop the noise; the challenge is not to allow noise power to take control of us. We become aware of the breathing, inner-space self in every moment. How do we know this is happening? We do not have to act, react or reply to someone's acts or words or the flood of impressions. We practice until we become aware of the inner space. We do not engage in unnecessary things like other people's arguments or yesterday's (or today's) news unless we choose to. When we do engage, we engage from the vision of the inner space.

Meditation 2: Let Go and Let God Exercise

In mystical meditation the practitioner must have a deep belief in the unique power and courage of the true spiritual self that 'Before I was, before my birth on earth, I existed.'

Coming to the freedom we had before we were born means we touch our ideal being. The soul is a sense of preexistence that we intuitively touch in meditation when the mind is receptive.

Self-help, self-control and self-esteem come from self-honesty and acceptance. It demands that our identity is not grounded on our material or social identity. We discover our identity by means of an existential awareness.

I receive existential serenity to the extent that I practice mind releasing. We touch the original self. We move from a worldly to a spiritual understanding. To let or let be is the issue.

The 'existential willingness' removes the dams around our inner being. It opens itself to persons, places and things by exercising spiritual receptivity.

'The truth is that knowledge is caused by the knower containing a likeness of the thing known; for the latter must be in the knower somehow' (Thomas Aquinas).

The existential horizon must become operational, and this is the function of the will. In meditative detachment we are delivered to true self. In the interior of our soul, we discover unsurpassable intimacy. There is power in the mind beyond time and space. 'In that power, God is fully verdant and flowering.' In the peak of the mind God lives and has always lived. When the mind is cleared it makes room for spiritual ideas. Calm detachment and courageous acceptance of the true self leads to a new birth of ideas and actions.

Method

Sit in a relaxed meditative position and begin to focus on your breathing with the counting practice of 1, 2, ... The lighting of a candle and appropriate meditative music is useful. Meditate for 10, 15 or 20 minutes. Practice this meditation rather frequently.

Use the mantra 'Let Go, Let God.' Inhale on 'Let Go' and exhale on 'Let God.' You may want to reverse this mantra at times to 'Let God, Let Go.' In the first mantra we call forth the inner Christ, the God, by releasing barriers to the soul. In the second breathing we are more focused on bringing God in and breathing out the ungodly.

Meditation 3: The Inner Christ

In Christian Zen, meditation is primarily about entering into a presence with the ground of our being. It is entering into the presence of the driving voice or spiritual voice within us where we discover our spiritual energy. In Christian Zen teaching, it is held that the essential source of this spiritual energy and vitality is found by entering into a presence with the inner Christ. The purpose of meditation is to take us from ego consciousness to meditative states of awareness as we advance into a Christ mindfulness: 'If you have any encouragement from being united with Christ, if any comfort from his love, if any fellowship with the Spirit, if any tenderness and compassion, then make my joy complete by being likeminded, having the same love, being one in spirit and purpose' (Philippians 2:1–2 NIV).

In Christian Zen meditation, we enter into our unique, existential and divine destiny, and we experience the stirring of God's love in the core of our being. It is at the existential core where we discover the ground of our being as we repeat the words 'I Am.'

The discovery of vitality and divine energy is a gift from God, and it is never depleted, limited or destroyed. Vitality is the enthusiastic embracing of life and living in a condition of hope and courage. Vitality, filled with enthusiasm and energy, means the same thing. In meditation, we intensely move to the inner, vital life and the flow of the Spirit.

Understanding the spiritual concept of mind is absolutely critical to the practice of meditation. No one has ever seen Mind or Spirit. The only proof we have is that we think, but we are perfectly justified in believing that we have a mind. In terms of the spiritual mind, there is no such thing as your mind and my mind, her mind and God's mind. There is just the spiritual mind (God's Mind) in which we live, move and have our being. Mind is both conscious and subconscious. The spiritual mind is our higher mind. The mind is potential divine energy, and thoughts and mood become a dynamic force that empowers our will. It is in the spiritual mind that we contact the mind of Christ.

Will means decision-making coming into execution. To will is to determine by an act of choice. The will is fundamental to living a spiritual life because without the activation of will we lose hope. Meditation leads us to the spiritual will and intuitive knowledge, rather than the rational will and knowledge. The will, truly, exists in the soul where we encounter spiritual mind and will. Therefore, we gain willpower when the divine force of the spiritual mind is joined with our decision.

Sit in a relaxed meditative position and practice breathing 1, 2, ... and then begin the mantra 'Thy Will, My Will.' It is in this meditation that our will and God's will merge. Use this meditation very frequently, sitting or walking, for 10, 15 or 20 minutes.

Meditation 4: 'Chris-te'
Method

The practice of Christian Zen is fundamentally a Christian way of being spiritual. It does not require that anyone accept any institutional dogmatic or systematic theology. Indeed, it is a method that avoids the serious limitations of much theological language.

Yet, it has a firm belief in the existence of the inner Christ. This belief in the inner Christ can be ontological in that a person holds Jesus Christ as a true and existing transcendental being of pure spirit and love who reigns above space and time in a heavenly domain. Or many hold that every human being has within their nature a participation in the Christ nature. Therefore, Christ in man means the idea of Sonship, the Perfect Man, as He must be held in the Mind of God. Christ within each and all.

'Christe' is the Greek word for Christ. It is a good word to use in meditation because it is from an ancient language of Christianity, e.g. Kyrie Eleison, Christe Eleison means 'Lord have mercy, Christ have mercy.'

Sit with the body and hands in a relaxed and meditative position. Break the word into 'Chris-' (the inhaling breath) '-te' (on the exhaling breath). Meditate for 10, 15, 20 minutes or longer. In this meditation, you may choose to repeat as a mantra: 'Lord have mercy, Christ have mercy.'

19

Five Christian Zen Reflections

One with Christ, Others and the World

With the practice of Christian Zazen (meditation), we begin to experience the presence of the inner Christ as the driving force behind all of creation. It is the 'metaphysical poets' who express beautifully the meaning of Divine Unity. Here is a quote from William Blake:

> To see a world in a grain of sand
> And heaven in a wild flower,
> Hold infinity in the palm of your hand
> And eternity in an hour.

Christ is the Son of God who is the living source of creation, i.e. the living energy of God's love. We must realize that even before the beginning of time and space, as we understand time and space, the Christ existed. The Son of God is not above the Father's world; the Son of God is the created universe. It is the universe that comes into existence as an expression of God's loving, creative and dynamic nature. We learn in Christian revelation clearly and without any ambiguity the nature of God. We learn in John that 'God is love, and those who abide in love abide in God, and God abides in them' (1 John 4:16 NRSV). Christ, therefore, is the creative energy and mind behind all of creation. Christ is the ultimate expression of our evolutionary nature. It is by means of the inner Christ that we understand the movement of the universe and our participation in the mystery of the Father's creation.

'*To see a world in a grain of sand*' is a fundamental principle of the spiritual/mystical life enlightened by the truth of the inner light. Christ is not only in every part of reality, but it is Christ who brings life into a greater whole. Everything and everyone in the world interacts even though this interaction is for the greater part invisible to our earthly observations. Each day everything is given creative meaning because it is in the nature of the Creator to continue creating. The Son of God has not finished His creation. Indeed, it is against the nature of God to stop creating because God is the creative and loving mind of the universe.

We must, therefore, get over our fragmented, isolated way of perceiving the world. When we look upon 'the grain of sand,' we must realize that we share our existence with the grain of sand. Even the smallest part of God's creation is there for the purpose of man's completeness. The human identity requires that I see my personality as sharing with the grain of sand. It means that our life in Christ is basically an ecological existence. Therefore, when man destroys the 'grains of sand,' he destroys his own existence. The exterior created world is not a reality exterior to the presence of man. The 'grains of sand' and man are one and the same. Just think of it this way: That used Coke can that we throw in the street is the 'grain of sand,' and it is a sacred act of worship when we recycle the can for the purpose of enhancing God's creation.

'And heaven in a wild flower' teaches us that creation must have symmetry. God means for all things and persons to have balance and beauty. It does not matter from which perspective one looks at a flower; the flower always maintains its symmetry. It must also be the same with God's universe and humanity. It is in the nature of evolution that we evolve to a higher state of symmetry. The world must evolve into a universal expression of beauty. It furthermore means that humanity must steadily evolve to have a more common appearance.

The power of the experience of the inner Christ is that we begin to get a small glimpse of heaven. We begin to experience heaven when we get a sense of balance, harmony and beauty. Therefore, we know something about our heavenly destiny when we experience a wonderful work of art, or grasp the meaning of the laws of physics, or read a truly human novel. We begin to grasp the nature of heaven when we have thoughts of beauty, harmony and balance running through our minds.

In a Christ consciousness, we sense the ultimate solution to world suffering and poverty, and it is in divine symmetry. It means that every part of the universe must explore what is shared in common. It is an attack on God's principle of symmetry when we exaggerate the differences of humanity. More and more, the world must rise to a new state of universal consciousness. We are no longer Christian, Jew or Muslim. We are no longer North American, South American, European, Asian, etc. Through the power and grace of the inner Christ we will continue to move to a 'global consciousness.' It is the principle of symmetry.

'Hold infinity in the palm of your hand' is a profound poetic statement that Christ does not come to us from the outside. It means that we are the Christ. It means that in our body Christ is in the cells, waiting for expression in our lifestyle. The Orthodox mystic St. Isaac the Syrian wrote, 'That is the Jerusalem or Kingdom of God hidden within us, according to the word of the Lord. Try to enter the cell within you, and you will see the heavenly cell. They are one and the same. By one entry you enter both. The ladder to the Heavenly Kingdom is within you. It is built mysteriously in your soul.'

When we look at our hands, we see the Kingdom of God. When we look at the palms of our hands we behold the New Jerusalem or the Kingdom of God. It is a type of heresy to expect the Kingdom of God to become anything other than what has begun in the palms of our hands. It is for this reason that Christ rose from the dead so that he could teach us that everybody is moving to the spiritual level. In a real sense, there is something rather beautiful to a hand as it ages. When the hand begins to age, it has a certain dignity because it teaches us that the cells of our body are truly spiritual.

'*And eternity in an hour*' means that life is short, but it is always rich in the presence of the inner Christ. When a Christian is asked, 'What will it be like in heaven?' the answer is, 'I expect it is something like the heaven within me.' We are the hour of eternity. In the practice of Christian Zen, we strive to live in a state of mindfulness. That is, we struggle to enter into Christ mindfulness in meditation, prayer, and our daily activities. It is the teaching of the mystic Brother Lawrence in *The Practice and Presence of God*:

> We might accustom ourselves to a continual conversation with Him with freedom and in simplicity. We need only to recognize God intimately present with us and address ourselves to Him every moment. We need to beg His assistance for knowing His will in things doubtful and for rightly performing those which we plainly see He requires of us, offering them to Him before we do them, and giving Him thanks when we have completed them.

In Christian Zen the concept of mindfulness and Christ presence are one and the same. It is when we enter into mindfulness that we experience 'eternity in an hour.'

Hearing the Loving Voice of the Inner Christ

In John 10, we read, 'The works that I do in my Father's name testify to me; but you do not believe, because you do not belong to my sheep. My sheep hear my voice. I know them, and they follow me. I give them eternal life, and they will never perish. No one will snatch them out of my hand' (John 10:25–28 NRSV).

This image that John uses of 'My sheep hear my voice' has given me cause to reflect upon the issue of: Just how do we hear the voice of God? I want to suggest that we must first know how to listen to the voice of the inner Christ if we wish to put into action the word of God.

At one of my weekly breakfast meetings with older fellow priests, we were talking about the difference between childhoods back then and now. We began this conversation because we were discussing the need for parents to keep in close contact with their children most of the time. We live in a society where the issues of security and protection always hang over our heads.

However, when we were children, we would simply go out into the streets and play all day. Maybe we would get on our bikes and just pedal around in and out the neighborhood all day. Today, such an idea is impossible to consider. We also recalled being called home for dinner by our parents. I would suggest that many people can still remember the call. In our exchange of memories, we smiled how each of us seemed still able to hear the unique and particular call of our parents. We could remember the particular call of, 'Ronnie, it's time for dinner' or 'It's time to come in.' One of the priests could remember his mother's powerful whistle. It was the uniqueness of the call and the sound of the parent's voice that we could easily remember. It was as if we could still hear it. It was as if the sound of the call to come in for the night was still in our body. In a sense the call by the loving parent to the children to come in for the night is an example of, 'I know mine and mine know me.'

As we reflected more on the parental request, we recalled that it was a clear and loving call, but the call also possessed a voice of authority. It was a beckoning from a loving parent, but it did demand a response to the authority of the call. As a matter of fact, there were usually levels to the authority of the call. The first one was a gentle call home such as, 'Ronnie, dinnertime.' However, sometimes Ronnie was involved in an interesting game of pick-up baseball, and after hearing the call he tended to ignore it. Then the second call came, and it was a little louder with more of a ring of authority: 'Ronnie, come in; it's getting dark and dinner is ready!' At this point, Ronnie could make a chancy decision and decide to ignore the second call. Then came the final authoritative call: 'Ronnie, did you hear me? Come in right now!' Ronnie was loved by his parents and his parents knew that they were responsible for the child. Consequently, the voice of the parent was the voice of a loving and nurturing parent, but it always had authority.

It is the same with the voice of the inner Christ. The voice of the inner Christ is always a loving call that comes to us in the midst of the play of life. It comes to us throughout the activities of the day. The call to prayer and meditation is like that of a parent when it is time to come in for the night. The voice of the inner Christ calling us to prayer and meditation is the most basic call of the day. It is a call to a nurturing and loving dialogue where we discover the voice of our soul. Still, it is a loving authoritative call just like that of the parent to the child when it is time to come home. We are called by the inner Christ to pray and meditate because He knows that it is for our own protection and nurturing.

The key issue is that the most straightforward way we hear the voice of the inner Christ is in the silence of our soul, our spiritual home. The truth of God is revealed to us in a special voice that comes to us when we are restful, calm and respectful of the needs of the inner soul. When we are calm and listen to the inner voice of Christ and ponder in prayer and obedience the thought patterns of our mind, we discover the truth of the inner Christ. We are never really living a spiritual life until we come to our inner self where we hear the thoughts of the Christ voice that move us to thoughtful concerns that lead us to action.

This voice of the inner Christ is the voice of a loving authority comprised of two extraordinary truths. One, we must give careful attention to the voice in our life because God knows who we are. It is not important that we know who we are; rather, we enter into conversation so that God will tell us who we are. It is in dialogue with the inner Christ that we discover our existential horizon.

The second truth is that we must hear the voice of Christ to know ourselves for who we are not. Hearing the voice of the Shepherd means we have entered into the divine conversation, and the main purpose is to know ourselves for who we are not and what we are able to become. This is the foundation of all spiritual authority; Christ knows us for who we are and He accepts us; in return, He lets us know what we are not and must become.

Deuteronomy 30:19–20 says, 'Now choose life, so that you and your children may live and that you may love the LORD your God, listen to his voice, and hold fast to him' (NIV). Here we have the promise of fully functioning and joyful life if we respect and follow the loving voice of the inner Christ. It is a voice like the voice we heard as children when we heard our parents call us to come in. It was a loving and nurturing voice, but it had an existential sound to it where we seem to find the ground of our being.

The Narrow Gate of Existential Heroism

Recently, I was listening to a friend in his early forties describing a terrifying experience as a mountain climber. I know this person and he is an excellent and competitive athlete. As a matter of fact, he still competes in tennis, but he is also an outdoors hunting and fishing type. It is his love of the outdoors and the emotional and physical challenge of sports that drew him to mountain climbing. He was introduced to the sport by his father-in-law who is a highly respected climber. His father-in-law is seventy-one, and he is a physician. He introduced his son-in-law to the sport, and he fell in love with it. The new mountain-climber found an outdoor sport that he loved, and he began to realize that the real drawing power of competition is against oneself. It is the climber against the mountain, and the climber must confront all his inner physical and emotional limitations.

The new climber approached the climbing sport with a type

'A' personality intensity. He was coached by his father-in-law, and he progressed quickly. He trained and slowly gained confidence despite his frailty as a climber. He loved the sport, and his trainer pointed out that he was a natural born mountain climber. After building his skills and confidence, the son and father-in-law decided to travel to climb a mountain in Argentina. They had picked a mountain of a moderate degree of difficulty. The new climber came to the foot of the mountain with a tremendous sense of confidence and excitement. It was a beautiful, almost perfect, day for climbing. With a confident attitude, they began the climb.

When they were about at the halfway point to the peak, the weather began to change. It quickly became overcast, and soon it went from dark and windy to extremely windy, and the rain became thunderous. Immediately, the quiet mountain had become treacherous. The new climber became overtaken by anxiety. Furthermore, he began to experience extreme nausea, and his body just seemed to be collapsing. He and his father-in-law sought immediate shelter in a rather narrow cave that was still in a dangerous location given the mountain weather conditions. It hit him that they were in a perilous and life-threatening situation. As he told the story, I could sense that he was almost reliving the menacing situation. 'Yes,' he said, 'I was afraid of losing my life.' His father-in-law, who is the seasoned climber and a physician, looked at him and said, 'You look fine. I can tell as a doctor and a seasoned climber that you can continue. Stay calm, follow me and we will make it. Let's keep going because it is more dangerous to stay here. Trust me and go with me to the top.'

As they continued in their climb, the sun once again appeared and the weather cleared. The seasoned climber did not panic because he had faced similar conditions in the past, and he knew that the weather often changed dramatically. The new climber described how they eventually reached the top of the mountain.

When they arrived the weather had become bright, calm and sunny. The view was awesomely beautiful. The new climber turned to his father-in-law, raised his arms and said, 'I feel like Rocky. I feel like a hero.'

In Luke 13, we read, 'Strive to enter through the narrow door; for many, I tell you, will try to enter and will not be able ... Then people will come from east to west, from north and south, and will eat in the kingdom of God. Indeed, some are last who will be first, and some are first who will be last' (Luke 13:24, 29–30 NRSV).

The narrow door represents the moments and occasions in our life when we are asked to confront, accept and face a demanding spiritual challenge. Often there are times in our lives when we must enter through a narrow door. It is when we are asked to exercise the courage to climb the mountain to the top, even though we are overtaken by the difficulty of the call to enter and walk through the narrow door. We will face occasions in life that become too much for us to handle or understand, and yet we must, in love, trust and faith, walk through the narrow door. When we walk through the narrow door, we discover that we are called in faith to be a hero.

Let us ask ourselves what narrow doors are calling us to enter. Where is it that the inner Christ wants us to climb? I was speaking with a Christian woman for whom I have much respect. She has a Master's in public administration, and she decided to get her Ph.D. in this field. She is very spiritual; she felt that public administration is her ministry, and she could be more effective in her call to a social justice ministry with her doctorate. She began her studies in a doctoral program that is very demanding in quantitative skills. She had been an 'A' student, but she was way over her natural abilities in the advanced statistics and algebra courses. She felt called by God, but she realized that she had entered a narrow door. She wondered why she had taken this path. She continued because she believed that

God wanted her to complete the task. She was like the mountain climber who became scared halfway through the journey. She continued, even as she discovered her limits, and she graduated a much better person. She graduated more humble in the Lord, ready for a new and powerful ministry.

In life, we are called frequently in Christ to enter through the narrow door because God wants us to discover the power of the spiritual and moral heroic aspect that exists within us. It is as Ralph Waldo Emerson wrote: 'The characteristic of heroism is its persistency. All men have wandering impulses, fits and starts of generosity. But when you have chosen your part, abide by it, and do not weakly try to reconcile yourself with the world. The heroic cannot be the common, nor the common the heroic.' Luke teaches us that we never discover the power of the heroic by going to religious laws that exist outside of our consciousness; we must enter the narrow gate where we confront our inner fears and doubts. It is when we enter the narrow gate that we truly meet the inner Christ on the heroic climb to the top of the mountain.

At the end of World War Two, in an upper room of a Dutch house where a Jew had been hiding for some time, a personal creed had been written on the wall. It is a creed that expresses the existential heroic aspect even when a person is living in an atmosphere of complete anxiety. As this person sat in this lonely place, living in fear of capture and the death camps, he found the inner power of his/her heroic soul and wrote:

I believe in the Sun even if it's not shining.
I believe in Love even if I don't feel it.
I believe in God even if He is silent.
(Author unknown)

Define and Redefine Your Existential Horizon

It is absolutely essential in living a dynamic and highly effective spiritual life that we are constantly in the process of defining and redefining our life. The willingness to engage in serious self-introspection is a necessary requirement to having a dynamic, Spirit-filled life. By 'dynamic,' I mean that we have a clear sense of living and continuously moving in a meaningful and fulfilling direction. It is the process of discovering our existential horizon.

It is a life that we are excited about, and we feel the energy of this excitement in all the affairs and activities of our existence. In other words, we are a people who are living an exciting and fully actualized existence. There is no book throughout the pages of scripture that draws our attention more to the issue of intro-spection than the book of Ecclesiastes. Before looking at Ecclesiastes, it is necessary to explain the meaning of a life of existential introspection.

If we want to know the advantages of living a spiritual life in Christ, then we must develop the habit of spiritual introspection. It means that we are prepared to conduct a spiritual inventory about the direction of our life. It simply means that we ask questions like, 'Why am I feeling bored?' 'Why does life feel so draining?' 'Why do I feel so pulled in so many different direc-tions? 'Why I am not excited about my life?' 'Why do I feel like I am really going nowhere with my life?' These are not in and of themselves bad questions or feelings; rather, they are issues critical to advancing in the spiritual life. They are the questions and feelings of life; if we address them by means of spiritual introspection then they will lead us to a more exciting and actualized life.

It means that we must on occasions take time to define our life as to where we are presently, and then redefine our life as to where we feel God is leading us. When we enter into spiritual introspection, we learn that we too easily define our life by the external events and situations of our life. Since our life is defined by the outward criteria of our existence, we quickly become carried away with our ego-driven accomplishments. When we live a non-spiritual life, we spend our time focusing on our achievements, earning praise and recognition and seeking approval.

If we ask someone, 'What are the great accomplishments of your life?' they will list the achievement of long-term goals, earning money, winning a game, getting a promotion and earning praise. It is always an emphasis on external events. We mention the things that happened outside of ourselves. There is nothing wrong with these accomplishments, but we learn from the book of Ecclesiastes that the outer accomplishments do not lead to a spiritual and deeply satisfying life. The teacher in Ecclesiastes explains: 'I, the Teacher, when king over Israel in Jerusalem, applied my mind to seek and to search out by wisdom all that is done under heaven; it is an unhappy business that God has given to human beings to be busy with. I saw all the deeds that are done under the sun; and see, all is [meaningless] and a chasing after wind' (Ecclesiastes 1:12–14 NRSV).

Here we learn the necessity of gaining wisdom by means of spiritual introspection. We must apply our minds, seek and search. The Teacher then warns us that if we search for happiness in external events then we will never find true spiritual happiness. In some translations the word 'vanity' is used, e.g. 'All is vanity and chasing after the wind.' Most scripture scholars today would agree that the Teacher's lesson is best conveyed by translating 'vanity' as 'meaningless,' and it is a word in Hebrew that can also be translated as 'breath' or 'vapor.' I find the word 'vapor' very helpful in grasping the Teacher's lesson. The external life, no matter how intense and temporarily exciting, is always merely a passing vapor. The Teacher pursues pleasure, but it is really a passing vapor. He attempts to find happiness in the various escapes and addictive practices of life – to no avail. Even the great accomplishments of building a business, creating a work of art, embracing the natural beauty of the universe, finding a wonderful job and gaining many possessions are all meaningless. He writes, 'What do mortals get from all the toil and strain with which they toil under the sun?' (Ecclesiastes 2:22 NRSV).

Wisdom, we learn, comes from our spiritual accomplishments that occur on the inside of the self. Spiritual meaning comes when we are kind and compassionate to ourselves and to others. It is when we have not over-reacted to a situation, but remained calm and loving. It is when we learned that we did not have to hold on to our anger. It is when we were able to let go and forgive others. It is the teaching of Ecclesiastes that the true measure of our happiness comes not from what we do, but from who we are and how much love we have in our hearts.

Therefore, life is the process of defining just where we are in life and asking ourselves if we are really living a life that is happy, joyous and free. Unless we are prepared to engage in spiritual introspection, we will always feel that our life is incomplete, no matter how great or beautiful our outer achievements. I have always been amazed by the practice of Buddhist monks in creating out of sand incredibly beautiful and complicated mandalas. They are the beautiful circles the monks meticulously create that express the harmony and sacredness of the universe. As soon as the mandala is completed, the monks wipe it away. I believe that this Buddhist practice captures the teaching of Ecclesiastes. Even the most beautiful and sacred external creations are like vapor in that all meaning and wisdom is only found with the internal sense of the power that created the beauty.

In Luke 12, Jesus deepens the lesson of Ecclesiastes that our meaning and happiness in life is not achieved by storing up accomplishments; rather, it is grounded on a life that treasures, more than anything else, an intense and personal spiritual relationship with God: 'You fool! This very night your life is being demanded of you. All the things you have prepared, whose will they be? So it is with those who store up treasures for themselves but are not rich towards God' (Luke 12:20–21 NRSV).

So, let us ask ourselves: Just what do we wish to accomplish this coming week, and why? Every time we ask this question, we are beginning our week with the process of spiritually defining and redefining our life.

Be a Spiritually Calm Super-Achiever

An intense and stressful job in the private sector is being a 'project manager.' This job is extremely nerve-racking in certain industries, especially with costly programs that must hit specific target dates. The ability to define these target dates and keep everything moving on a cost schedule is the function of the project manager. Good project scheduling and management is especially important with new product development in manufacturing and engineering projects. The project manager must have a high level of expert knowledge about the technical issues involved, a keen sense of cost accounting issues, a masterful use of computer technology and strong people skills. If I could pick one overriding characteristic of a project manager, I would say that it is the ability to remain calm under stress. In other words, the manager has the ability to remain calm under fire and still motivate people.

One of the best project managers I have ever known is a friend, Marty. I have discovered in life that some of our closest friends are individuals we stood alongside under fire. Marty was an outstanding technical project manager. He was the best I have ever known at planning out the engineering steps of a project and setting reasonable target dates, but it was his people skills that most impressed me. Marty is a deeply spiritual man with a gentle sense of humor that he would often use to resolve conflict situations. His spiritual bent was often expressed in his ability to patiently listen to people, often letting them rant and rave about the issues. He would listen to the conflicting views, summarize, give calm feedback and lead to a resolution. It was his spiritual talents of gentleness, listening and feedback being used in a pressured work environment that always amazed me. It is for these reasons that Marty still lives a deeply spiritual Christian life, and he is now an important manager with a large American corporation.

I want to suggest that we might look at life as an issue of project management under stress. We have our challenges, pressures and the financial issues of life, but we may manage life better if we are a type of spiritual and calm project manager. A reason many of us remain hurried, frightened and competitive and live as if life were one great emergency is that we lack spiritual calmness. We believe that if we are not driven, especially in the work force, we will be seen as lazy and apathetic. It is the issue that we confront in the gospel story of Martha and Mary (Luke 10:38–42). The scene takes place in the home of Martha and Mary where Jesus spent a great deal of time. It is the narrative of the two sisters. Martha welcomed Jesus into their home, and she is the driven project manager. She is the one who is driven as a hurried multi-task manager. She perceives her sister as too laidback. Martha is angry that her sister is not more like her, and Mary, on the other hand, sees her major priority as sitting calmly at the feet of Jesus and listening. Martha sees herself as needing to act as the super-achiever. She sees her sister as lazy and apathetic, but the gospel narrative tells us that Mary is the *real* super-achiever; more precisely she is a real spiritual super-achiever. Fearful, frantic thinking takes an enormous amount of emotional energy and drains the creativity and motivation from our lives. We immobilize ourselves when we are hurried, fearful and frantic, and we are unable to sense reality and realize the possibilities of life. Consequently, any success we have is despite our fears and frenzied lifestyle. One of the blessings of life is to have had the experience of knowing and learning from calm, relaxed, peaceful and loving people. Furthermore, many of our bestselling authors, spiritual writers, saints, scholars' teachers, counselors, clergy and parents etc. are filled with the spiritual calmness of Mary. We need the spiritual calmness of Mary in every aspect of our lives, namely family, vocational, leisure and lifestyle.

Let me ask some simple Martha/Mary type questions. For example, who would you choose for a trustworthy friend: Martha, the highly driven, frantic super-achiever; or Mary, the spiritual super-achiever? Who would a person choose to work for: a hurried, uptight Martha or a spiritually calm Mary? Who would you choose to look after your estate? Who would you chose for a doctor: a doctor who is frantically running from patient to patient, or a calm and caring healer?

This narrative is rather clear in the establishment of our life orientation as practitioners of Christian Zen because Jesus says, 'Martha, Martha, you are worried and distracted by many things; there is need of only one thing. Mary has chosen the better part, which will not be taken away from her' (Luke 10:41–42 NRSV). Jesus here is telling us that we must manage our life from our spiritual center which is the place where we listen to the voice of Christ within our consciousness. It is the inner place where we sit quietly in centering prayer and meditation and listen to the voice of our Savior.

I want to suggest that this story of Martha and Mary also describes the nature of the spiritual mind. God has created us as spiritual and material beings. In the material ego of the brain and body we will always become frantic and driven by the challenges and pressures of our life. Even many Christians, who have not discovered the emotional and spiritual tranquility of Jesus, remain in their materialistic driven ego of the mechanical brain and body. Spiritual Christians choose the Mary dimension of their personality where they quietly listen to the inner voice of their soul and mind. This is the meaning of Jesus' teaching: 'Mary has chosen the better part, which will not be taken away from her.' As a result, the narrative asks us to choose between our limited Martha nature, and our enlightened Mary mind. We can continue to constantly worry about tomorrow. We can continue the frantic pace of life. We can let our emotional and physical health break down from worry. We can rush about and isolate ourselves from others in our own little world, or we can choose 'the better part.'

References

Allen, James. *As a Man Thinketh*, 1992.

Barrett, William. *Irrational Man: A Study in Existential Philosophy.* New York: Doubleday Anchor Books, 1958.

Damasio, Antonio. *Looking for Spinoza: Joy, Sorrow and the Feeling Brain.* Harcourt, 2003.

French, Hal. *Zen and the Art of Anything.* Broadway Books, 1999.

Happold, F.C. *Mysticism: A Study and an Anthology.* Maryland: Penguin Books, 1963.

Heidegger, Martin. *Being and Time.* Translated by John Macquarrie and Edward Robinson. Harper Perennial, 1962.

Holmes, Ernest. *The Science of Mind: A Philosophy, A Faith, A Way of Life.* New York: Penguin Putnam, 1997.

Inwood, Michael. *Heidegger: A Very Short Introduction.* Oxford University Press, 1997.

Johnston, William. *Christian Zen: A Way of Meditation.* San Francisco: Harper & Row, 1979.

Kapleau, Philip. *The Three Pillars of Zen: Teaching, Practice and Enlightenment.* New York: Anchor Books, 1980.

Leong, Kenneth S. *The Zen Teachings of Jesus.* New York: Crossroads Publishing, 1995.

Mitchell, Stephen. *A New English Version, Tao Te Ching.* New York: Harper & Row, 1988.

May, Gerald G. *The Awakened Heart: Opening Yourself to the Love You Need.* San Francisco, HarperCollins, 1991.

May, Rollo. *The Courage to Create.* New York/London: W.W. Norton & Co, 1975.

Nowak, Paul. *The Way of the Christian Samurai.* 2005.

Polkinghorne, John. *The God of Hope and the End of the World.* Yale University, New Haven/ London, 2002.

Royce, Josiah. *The Problem of Christianity.* General-Books.net, 1913; reprint 2010.

Royce, Josiah. *The Sources of Religious Insight*. Charles Scribner Sons, 1912.

Sartre, Jean-Paul. *Existentialism and Human Emotions*. Wisdom Library, New York, 1957.

Snyder, C.R. *The Psychology of Hope: You Can Get There from Here*. Free Press, 1994.

Circle Books

Circle is a symbol of infinity and unity. It's part of a growing list of imprints, including o-books.net and zero-books.net.

Circle Books aims to publish books in Christian spirituality that are fresh, accessible, and stimulating.

Our books are available in all good English language bookstores worldwide. If you can't find the book on the shelves, then ask your bookstore to order it for you, quoting the ISBN and title. Or, you can order online—all major online retail sites carry our titles.

To see our list of titles, please view www.Circle-Books.com, growing by 80 titles per year.

Authors can learn more about our proposal process by going to our website and clicking on Your Company > Submissions.

We define Christian spirituality as the relationship between the self and its sense of the transcendent or sacred, which issues in literary and artistic expression, community, social activism, and practices. A wide range of disciplines within the field of religious studies can be called upon, including history, narrative studies, philosophy, theology, sociology, and psychology. Interfaith in approach, Circle Books fosters creative dialogue with non-Christian traditions.

And tune into MySpiritRadio.com for our book review radio show, hosted by June-Elleni Laine, where you can listen to authors discussing their books.

MySpiritRadio